365 GUIDE™

New York City

DRINK.EAT.$AVE.
EVERY DAY OF THE YEAR.™

MONICA DiNATALE

365 Guide
DRINK.EAT.$AVE. EVERY DAY OF THE YEAR.
MONICA DiNATALE

ISBN: 978-1-936449-47-7
LOCC: 2013941606

Original Logo Design: Deborah Hasselmark
Cover and Interior Design: DPMediaPro.com
New York City Subway Map © Metropolitan Transportation Authority. Used with permission.
Hugo House Publishers
Englewood, Colorado
877-700-0616
www.HugoHousePublishers.com

Hugo House

To contact the Author:
monicadinatale@aol.com
www.365guidenyc.com

Dedication

Thank you John Eureyecko for being my eating, drinking and life caddie. Without you *365 Guide* would not contain the same amount of joy and passion.

To locals and tourists alike, enjoy the savings and try to capture some of the spirit of New York City!

About The Author

Monica DiNatale, a 2007 Writer's Guild Award winner, is a New York City Food Host & Dining Deals Expert. Monica has been a featured Dining Expert for iFood.tv, The Frugalicious Show and Brick Underground NY. She has hosted segments for The New York Chocolate Show and The New York City Craft Beer Week Festival. Monica also produced *Fun Food with Monica,* receiving two million plus views, and Tweets deals daily on Twitter (@365guide).

You can follow Monica on Twitter and Facebook, and catch her favorite places and deals on everything from ice cream to computer discounts.

For more special discounts, submit your email on the home page of www.365guidenyc.com.

Monica's passion for eating, drinking and saving while living in New York City led to *365 Guide*.

www.365guidenyc.com
www.twitter.com/365guide
www.facebook.com/365guide

TABLE OF CONTENTS

The Greatest City in the World has often been called the Culinary Capital of the World, or, most famously, the City that Never Sleeps!

New York is a city of "finds." If you live here or if you're visiting, you inevitably will say at some point, "After a full day, we found this incredible place by accident," or, "we stumbled into this hidden gem for a drink." New York City is full of places where you and those you are with can share memorable drinks and satisfying meals at great places—and great prices!

What if you knew exactly where to go to enjoy these unique "finds" before your night started, or before you've even arrived in the Big Apple? What if you could plan a visit to a unique pub, or get a super "deal" for dinner, before you even left your home?

Great "finds" and super "deals" make for great memories, and this is what *365 Guide* is all about—a deal-a-day, every day of the year!

The density and diversity of a city eight million strong representing nearly every country in the world means that you'll never have a shortage of places to go. But where should you go? How much will it cost? Does it always have to be so expensive?

Many people come to New York City with the preconceived notion that drinking and eating is always a hassle and unaffordable. Without knowing where to eat, which neighborhood you're in, or which places are worth a visit, it can be frustrating. You need someone to show you where to look!

365 Guide details all you'll need to make eating and drinking in New York City fun, memorable, and yes, even affordable. Drink. Eat. Save. Every Day of the Year! *365 Guide* shares insider tips to help you navigate the city like a pro. Whether you're a first

MONICA DiNATALE

time visitor or a lifetime resident, with *365 Guide*, your time spent in Manhattan is sure to make you feel like you belong.

The entries here include all neighborhoods in Manhattan and guide you around popular landmarks. If you're looking for a restaurant near Times Square with free appetizers during happy hour, *365 Guide* can help you plan your evening. In addition, *365 Guide* highlights what each restaurant is known for, so you'll always know what to order.

Think of *365 Guide* as your personal entertainment concierge. From the best dive bars to exclusive five-star restaurants, *365 Guide* will lead you on a fun and economical adventure as you visit the best restaurants and bars in New York City. As a bonus, if you're just visiting, you'll also get to know the neighborhoods and be able to answer the question, "Where's the East Village?"

I once thought New York would be large, unmanageable, and overly expensive. When I first moved here I thought I'd last one year, enjoy the nightlife and the food, and leave here with some great memories. That was fifteen years ago! I'm still here, eating, drinking, and enjoying the best from every square inch of the city.

Throughout this time I've built incredible memories. I've eaten every kind of food imaginable, had drinks in the coolest places, and spent hours in the best of the "dives" talking to fun and interesting people. I've gone to the "in" places and I've found off-the-beaten-path places that only a local would know. Through it all, New York City has grabbed me completely, and I'll continue enjoying everything it has to offer.

I wish everyone living or visiting here the same joy and experiences with these a deal-a-day for every day of the year. Enjoy my 365 hidden gems to the fullest. And keep a lookout—there's a good chance I'll meet you there!

Cheers!
Monica DiNatale

HOW TO USE 365 GUIDE

To quality for inclusion in *365 Guide*, each bar/restaurant must be open for a minimum of five years and consistently offer customers savings!

You can find your "deal" searching by name, neighborhood, landmark or type of restaurant/bar. *365 Guide* makes it easy to find exactly what you are in the mood for.

Neighborhood listings give you an idea of which neighborhood the restaurant is closest to in order to make your search easier. You can also start your search by utilizing the Manhattan At-A-Glance map at the back of the book to pinpoint your location. If you're reading this electronically, with wifi, just click on the link, and you'll be directed to a web address or Google® map that shows you exactly where you need to go.

To get the most from your *365 Guide,* follow the guidelines below.

■ Log on to www.365guidenyc.com and follow *365 Guide* on Facebook and Twitter (@365guide) to receive the "find" of the day.

■ Types of wines, brands of beer, and specials offered can change at the discretion of the establishment. Those Strawberry Mojitos in summer will change to Eggnog Martinis in winter. But rest assured that all the restaurants and bars who are part of *365 Guide* know the value of offering customers a discount.

■ "Bar" and/or "Restaurant" descriptions mean an American-type food menu. Ethnic restaurants are listed as such.

■ Some of the specials listed in *365 Guide* are for bar seating only. Don't be afraid to ask your friendly bartender for food and drink specials. You will find

viii

that they are more than happy to share discounts with you.

■ Check the "Seasonal Finds" section to find great outdoor seating with water views in summer as well as holiday favorites and "Restaurant Week" promotions.

■ FREE food offerings are based on a beverage purchase.

■ Bars in New York that don't serve food will often let you order food from a nearby restaurant. Just ask. It is a nice way to keep costs down.

■ Most restaurants in New York offer "lunch specials" Monday through Friday. This is a great way to try a restaurant at a discounted price. Hours will vary but most lunch menus are over by 3p.m.

■ Many restaurants in New York offer a prix-fixe "brunch menu" on Saturdays and Sundays. You will find that a FREE alcoholic beverage, like a mimosa or a Bloody Mary, is often included in this price. Hours will vary but most brunch menus are done by 3 p.m.–4 p.m.

WHAT	DEAL	LOCATION
2A Bar	4 p.m.–8 p.m. daily $2 drafts, wine & well $3 bottles	25 Avenue A (at 2nd Street) 2 Av (F) Delancey St (F) Essex St (J, M, Z) EAST VILLAGE
DJ, projector for movies		
8th Street Wine Cellar Wine Bar	4 p.m.–7 p.m. daily $6 wine $18 bottles	28 West 8th Street (between 5th Avenue & MacDougal Street) W 4 St (A, B, C, D, E, F, M) Christopher St–Sheridan Sq (1, 2) 8 St–Nyu (N, R) THE VILLAGE
Wine tastings, private parties		
12th Street Ale House Bar	5 p.m.–8 p.m. daily $2.50 well $3.50 drafts	192 Second Avenue (at 12th Street) 3 Av (L) 1 Av (L) Astor Pl (4, 6, 6X) EAST VILLAGE
FREE bar nuts, jukebox		

MONICA DiNATALE

HOURS	CONTACT	365 EXTRAS
Daily 4 p.m.–4 a.m.	212-505-2466 www.2anyc.com	I like to sit upstairs in the lounge. The downstairs bar has just enough room to grab a drink and strike up a conversation. It's on the corner and lined with windows so it makes for great people watching.
Daily 4 p.m.–2 a.m.	212-260-9463 www.8thstwinecellar.com	Be careful not to walk by this sleek wine bar, hidden below the sidewalk. Order a cheese plate or wild mushroom bruschetta with an $18 bottle and settle in for a beautiful evening.
Mon–Fri 5 p.m.–2 a.m. Sat–Sun 4 p.m.–4 a.m.	212-253-2323	A great "dive bar" with a relaxed vibe and $6 craft beers any day of the week. Plenty of seating and good rock music. They get enthusiastic crowds for sporting events.

WHAT	DEAL	LOCATION
123 Burger Shot Beer Bar & Restaurant	Daily $1 burgers $2 shots $3 beers 11 a.m.–8 p.m. Monday–Friday ½ price well	738 Tenth Avenue (between 50th & 51st Streets) 50 St (1, 2, A, C, E) HELL'S KITCHEN/ MIDTOWN WEST
Sports specials, late night kitchen until 4 a.m.		
169 Bar Bar & Restaurant	1 p.m.–7:30 p.m. daily $1 off cans & drafts $2 off everything else $3 beer & shot	169 East Broadway (between Jefferson & Essex Streets) East Broadway (F) Grand & Chrystie Street (B) LOWER EAST SIDE
Pool table, private parties, DJ on weekends		
809 Sangria Bar & Grill Spanish/Latin American Restaurant	5 p.m.–9 p.m. Monday–Friday $4 appetizers $5 beer & wine $8 cocktails	112 Dyckman Street (between Nagle Ave & Post Avenue) Dyckman St (A, 1) 207 St (1) WASHINGTON HEIGHTS
Live music Fridays, dinner specials		

4

HOURS	CONTACT	365 EXTRAS
Daily 11 a.m.–4 a.m.	212-315-0123 www.123burger-shotbeer.com	The name says it all! The mini-burgers are awesome. I like the lemon drop and creamsicle shots. The food is reasonable in general and they offer party platters for big groups.
Mon–Sat 1 p.m.–4 a.m. Sun 4 p.m.–4 a.m.	212-641-0357 www.169barnyc.com	This place is inspired by New Orleans (the city, and the owner). Try the raw bar, an oyster shooter, or a hurricane. Jazz & soul sounds keep it fun and funky!
Mon–Thu 11a.m.–12 a.m. Fri 11a.m.–2 a.m. Sat 4 p.m.–2 a.m. Sun 12 p.m.–12 a.m.	212-304-3800 www.809restaurant.com	The restaurant is downstairs and provides a sophisticated Spanish vibe with a bright red décor and flavorful ceviche. Upstairs you'll find 809 Lounge, a club with DJ music. Swanky.

	WHAT	DEAL	LOCATION
7	**1020 Bar** Bar	Daily $2–$3 beer $4 well	**1020 Amsterdam Avenue** (between 111th Street & Cathedral Parkway) **Cathedral Pkwy (1)** **116 St–Columbia University (1)** **Cathedral Pkwy (110 St) (A, B, C)** **MORNINGSIDE HEIGHTS**
	Columbia University bar, pool table		
8	**1849** Bar & Restaurant	3 p.m.–6 p.m. daily ½ price beer & well until 8 p.m. daily $.55 wings; Tue: $3 Cuervo & Coronas 8 p.m.–1 a.m.; Wed: $7 pitchers; Thu: $.05 drafts with appetizer purchase, $3 drafts 8 p.m.–1 a.m.	**183 Bleecker Street** (between MacDougal & Sullivan Streets) **W 4 St (A, B, C, D, E, F, M)** **Houston St (1, 2)** **Spring St (A, C, E)** **THE VILLAGE**
	Fifteen plasmas, pool table, DJs, live music		
9	**Acqua at Peck Slip** Italian & Seafood Restaurant	2 p.m.–7 p.m. Monday–Friday $3 beer $6 wine & cocktails	**21 Peck Slip** (between Pearl & Water Streets) **Fulton St (2, 3)** **Fulton St (A, C, J, Z)** **Brooklyn Bridge–City Hall (4, 5, 6, 6X)** **SOUTH STREET SEAPORT**
	Outdoor seating, special occasion, dinner specials		

MONICA DiNATALE

HOURS	CONTACT	365 EXTRAS
Daily 4 p.m.–4 a.m.	212-531-3468	This is a no-frills corner neighborhood bar with booth seating, awesome prices and laid back ambience. It's easy to sip the day away with those prices. No food.
Mon–Wed 3 p.m.–4 a.m. Thu–Sun 12 p.m.–4 a.m.	212-505-3200 www.1849nyc.com	I absolutely love the red velvet chairs and tables in the front of the bar. Perfect for meeting friends or an intimate conversation. The menu has a Tex–Mex flair. Try the in-house smoked ribs or one of the many burgers.
Mon–Sat 12 p.m.–11 p.m. Sun 12 p.m.–10 p.m.	212-349-4433 www.acquarestaurantnyc.com	Perfectly picturesque Italian wine bar and restaurant with good pizzas and several homemade pastas. They make you feel at home. Try the bufalina pizza with pesto. Pastas range from $16–$22.

	WHAT	DEAL	LOCATION
10	**Adrienne's Pizza Bar** Italian Restaurant	4 p.m.–6 p.m. Monday–Friday $4 drafts $5 well	54 Stone Street (between Hanover Square & Coenties Alley) Broad St (J, Z) Whitehall St (N, R) Wall St (2, 3) FINANCIAL DISTRICT
	Reservations for six or more, outdoor seating		
11	**Agave** Mexican Restaurant	3 p.m.–7 p.m. daily ½ off margaritas, beer, wine $5 frozen margaritas	140 Seventh Avenue South (between Charles Street & 10th Street) Christopher St–Sheridan Sq (1, 2) W 4 St (A, B, C, D, E, F, M) 14 St (1, 2, 3) THE VILLAGE
	Prix-fixe specials, tequila menu		
12	**Agozar** Cuban Bistro & Bar	5 p.m.–8 p.m. daily, Mondays all night Buy-1-get-1- FREE drinks & tapas	324 Bowery (between Bleecker & Bond Streets) Bleecker St (4, 6, 6X) 2 Av (F) Broadway–Lafayette St (B, D, F, M) EAST VILLAGE
	Vegetarian menu, private parties		

8

HOURS	CONTACT	365 EXTRAS
Mon–Sat 11:30 a.m.–12 a.m. Sun 11:30 a.m.–10 p.m.	212-248-3838 www.adriennespizz-abar.com	Stone Street is one of my favorite places in this area. It is a brick lined pedestrian-only haven in an otherwise busy neighborhood. Try the calabrese with broccoli rabe and sausage or the square old fashioned pie.
Mon 12 p.m.–11 p.m. Tue–Fri 12 p.m.–1 a.m. Sat 11:30 a.m.–1 a.m. Sun 11:30 a.m.–11 p.m.	212-989-2100 www.agaveny.com	Upscale Mexican food in a modern bright setting with nothing but windows. Endless mimosas at brunch on weekends. Try the skirt steak fajitas. Agave doubles in size with tons of outdoor seating in nice weather.
Mon–Wed 12 p.m.–12 a.m. Thu 12 p.m.–1 a.m. Fri–Sat 12 p.m.–3 a.m. Sun 12 p.m.–10 p.m.	212-677-6773 www.agozarnyc.com	Amazing mojitos with ten different types; I like the sangrito. Bright orange walls and interesting artwork keep the atmosphere lively. Unique tapas like mole poblano grilled shrimp.

WHAT	DEAL	LOCATION
13 **Amity Hall** Bar & Restaurant	Until 7 p.m. Monday–Friday $5 craft beer, well & specials	80 West 3rd Street (between Thompson & Sullivan Streets) W 4 St (A, B, C, D, E, F, M) Christopher St–Sheridan Sq (1, 2) 8 St–Nyu (N, R) THE VILLAGE
Rotating dinner and drink specials, private parties, trivia nights		
14 **Amsterdam Ale House** Pub & Restaurant	4 p.m.–7 p.m. Monday–Friday $2 off domestic drafts $4 bottles $4 house high balls $5 wine	320 Amsterdam Avenue (at 76th Street) 79 St (1, 2) 72 St (1, 2, 3) 81 St–Museum of Natural History (A, B, C) UPPER WEST SIDE
Sports specials, fireplace, brewery events		
15 **Amsterdam Restaurant & Tapas Lounge** Bar & Restaurant	4 p.m.–7 p.m. Monday–Friday $2 Bud & Coors drafts $3 well $5 martinis, Cosmos & margaritas	1207 Amsterdam Avenue (between 119th & 120th Streets) 116 St (A, B, C, 1) 125 St (A, B, C, D) MORNINGSIDE HEIGHTS
10 Two floors with dancing downstairs, DJs on weekends		

HOURS	CONTACT	365 EXTRAS
Sun–Mon 12 p.m.–2 a.m. Tue–Sat 12 p.m.–4 a.m.	212-677-2290 www.amityhallnyc.com	Great bar food, burgers and pizzas. The bar area is spacious with plenty of seating for sporting events. Twenty beers on tap plus cask ale. They always offer discounted food deals.
Mon–Fri 11:30 a.m.–4 a.m. Sat–Sun 11 a.m.–4 a.m.	212-362-7260 www.amsterdamalehouse.com	Classic Irish pub feel with thirty one drafts and sixty five bottles. I am in love with the burgers and sweet potato fries and like to check out their visiting breweries. Quiet, cozy dining room in back with a fireplace.
Sun–Tue 11 a.m.–3 a.m. Wed–Sat 11 a.m.–4 a.m.	212-662-6330 www.amsterdamrestaurant.com	Near Columbia University, so prices are reasonable. I can recommend the burritos and the fish tacos. Outdoor sidewalk seating with bistro décor and a friendly staff.

WHAT	DEAL	LOCATION
Amsterdam Tavern Irish Pub	4 p.m.–7 p.m. Monday–Friday $2 off craft beers $4 wine $5 well	938 Amsterdam Avenue (between 106th & 107th Streets) 103 St (1, A, B, C) Cathedral Pkwy (1) UPPER WEST SIDE
Add $10 to brunch for unlimited Bloody Marys, mimosas or sangria from 12 p.m.–3 p.m. on weekends.		
Apple Restaurant and Bom Bar Vietnamese/Thai Restaurant	4 p.m.–7 p.m. Monday–Saturday ½ off drinks	17 Waverly Place (between Green & Mercer Streets) 8 St–Nyu (N, R) Astor Pl (4, 6, 6X) Bleecker St (4, 6, 6X) THE VILLAGE
Karaoke room, private party packages that include karaoke		
Arctica Restaurant & Bar	4 p.m.–9 p.m. Monday–Thursday, 12 p.m.–8 p.m. Friday $4 beers $6 cocktails & champagne	384 Third Avenue (between 27th & 28th Streets) 23 St, 28 St, 33 St (4, 6, 6X) FLATIRON/ GRAMERCY
$10–$14 brunch on weekends includes a FREE draft, Bloody Mary or mimosa.		

16

17

18

12

HOURS	CONTACT	365 EXTRAS
Sun–Mon 12 p.m.–3 a.m. Tue–Sat 12 p.m.–4 a.m.	212-280-8070 www.amsterdam-tavernnyc.com	The double bypass burger is worth it. Double the every-thing! The chorizo chili and falafel sliders are also worth trying. There are twenty plus beers on tap and some sweet martinis.
Mon–Thu 12 p.m.–11 p.m. Fri–Sat 12 p.m.–12 a.m.	212-473-8888 www.applerestau-rant.com	This place has a very tranquil right-out-of-Asia décor. The whole place is conducive to relaxing with friends. Try the black pearl martini. You can rent the karaoke room to become a rock star.
Mon–Fri 12 p.m.–4 a.m. Sat–Sun 11 a.m.–4 a.m.	212-725-4477 www.arcticabar.com	Try the watermel-on-tini and the straw-berry caipirinha. Diverse menu includes lobster ravioli and tacos. Sleek, modern, and narrow, with plenty of seating. Wednesdays are open-mic night.

| **19** **Arriba Arriba**
 Mexican Restaurant | 4 p.m.–7 p.m. Monday–Friday

 $5 "papa" margarita | 762 Ninth Avenue
 (at 51st Street)
 50 St (A, C, E, 1, 2)
 7 Av (B, D, E)

 HELL'S KITCHEN/ MIDTOWN WEST |

$8.95 lunch specials 12 p.m.–4 p.m. Monday–Friday, $12.95 brunch Saturday and Sunday 11 a.m.–4 p.m.

| **20** **Aroma Kitchen & Wine Bar**
 Italian Restaurant | 5 p.m.– 6:30 p.m. daily

 ½ off select wines by the glass & bottle

 $15 flight of three wines & appetizer | 36 East 4th Street
 (between Lafayette & Bowery Streets)
 Bleecker St (4, 6, 6X)
 Astor Pl (4, 6, 6X)
 8 St-Nyu (N, R)

 EAST VILLAGE/ NOHO |

Homemade pastas, good for a date

| **21** **Art Bar**
 Bar | 5 p.m.–7 p.m. daily

 ½ price drafts, wine, well | 52 Eighth Avenue
 (between Jane & Horatio Streets)
 8 Av (L)
 14 St (A, C, E, 1, 2, 3)

 THE VILLAGE |

Fireplace, jukebox, local artist gallery

MONICA DiNATALE

HOURS	CONTACT	365 EXTRAS
Mon–Thu 12 p.m.–12 a.m. Fri 12 p.m.– 1 a.m. Sat 11 a.m.– 1 a.m. Sun 11 a.m.– 12 a.m.	212-489-0810 www.arribaarrib-awest.com	A good spot for frozen margaritas and fresh guacamole. They offer large portions, outdoor seating and authentic Mexican dinner entrees. I love the fajitas.
Mon–Thu, Sun 5 p.m.–12 a.m. Fri–Sat 5 p.m.–1 a.m.	212-375-0100 www.aromanyc.com	Beautiful oak and wine filled rustic Italian gem. Try one of the homemade pastas or any of the nightly specials. The cavatelli with an oxtail ragu are amazing. Small and romantic.
Daily 4 p.m.–4 a.m.	212-727-0244 www.artbar.com	I like the fireplace in the back lounge with comfy couches and the large booths at the bar. Fun seasonal drinks like a pumpkin pie martini. The casual menu includes burgers, wraps and sandwiches.

	WHAT	DEAL	LOCATION
22	**Ashton's Alley** Bar & Restaurant	5 p.m.–7 p.m. Monday–Friday $5 wine, beer & well	825 Third Avenue (at 50th, between 2nd & 3rd Avenues) 51 St (4, 6, 6X) Lexington Av/53 St (E, M) 5 Av/53 St (E, M) MIDTOWN EAST
	Twenty HD TVs, two hours of unlimited drinks at brunch on weekends		
23	**Asia Roma (AR Restaurant)** Asian/Roman Restaurant	3 p.m.–7 p.m. Monday–Friday $1 appetizers $3–$4 beer $5 cocktails & shots	40 Mulberry Street (between Bayard & Worth Streets) Canal St (J, N, Q, Z) Chambers St (J, Z) Brooklyn Bridge–City Hall (4, 5, 6, 6X) CHINATOWN
	Karaoke, private parties		
24	**B Flat** Bar & Restaurant	5 p.m.–8 p.m. daily $4 beer $5 wine $7 cocktails appetizer specials	277 Church Street, basement (between White and Franklin Streets) Franklin St (1, 2) Canal St (A, C, E, N, R) TRIBECA
	Live jazz Monday and Wednesday from 8 p.m.–11 p.m.		

MONICA DiNATALE

HOURS	CONTACT	365 EXTRAS
Mon–Sun 11:30 a.m.– 2 a.m. Tue–Sat 11:30 a.m.– 4 a.m.	212-688-8625 www.ashtonsalleysportsbar.com	This place attracts a power crowd after work. Although it's a sports bar, it maintains a cool New York atmosphere. The American menu includes everything from salads to filet mignon.
Mon–Thu 11:30 a.m.– 2 a.m. Fri 11:30 a.m.– 4 a.m. Sat 5 p.m.–4 a.m.	212-385-1133 www.asiaroma.com	Sing your heart out and become a legend at the downstairs karaoke den. Great for a group looking to have fun! Italian–Asian mix of food. I like that I can order vegetable spring rolls and clams casino.
Mon–Wed 5 p.m.–2 a.m. Thu–Sat 5 p.m.–3 a.m.	212-219-2970 www.bflat.info	Just look for the red doors! I love the low–key vibe with a jazzy beat and interesting mixed drinks. All the seating is intimate so settle in for a nice evening. Try the giant steps martini with wasabi flavored vodka.

365 GUIDE New York City

	WHAT	DEAL	LOCATION
25	**B Side** Bar	3 p.m.–8 p.m. daily $2 off beer ½ price well	204 Avenue B (between 12th & 13th Streets) 1 Av (L) 3 Av (L) EAST VILLAGE
	Jukebox, foosball		
26	**Back Forty** Restaurant & Bar	Monday 6 p.m.–Close, Tuesday–Thursday 6 p.m.–8 p.m., Friday 6 p.m.–7 p.m., Saturday 2:30 p.m.–7 p.m., Sunday 3 p.m.–7 p.m. ½ price drinks	190 Avenue B (at 12th Street) 1 Av, 3 Av (L) EAST VILLAGE
	Oyster specials Saturdays, 4 p.m.–5:30 p.m. and Sundays, 3:30 p.m.–5:30 p.m.		
27	**Baker Street Pub** Irish Pub	11 a.m.–7 p.m. Monday–Friday Buy-1-get-1-FREE well, wine, beer	1152 First Avenue (at 63rd Street) Lexington Av/63 St (F) Lexington Av/59 St (N, Q, R) Roosevelt Island (F) UPPER EAST SIDE
	Featured in the 1988 movie "Cocktail"		

MONICA DiNATALE

HOURS	CONTACT	365 EXTRAS
Daily 3 p.m.–4 a.m.	212-475-4600	It's small with a larger room in the back that has a foosball table. They always have $3–$4 beers. One of those places that is comfortable like your own living room.
Sun–Wed 6 p.m.– 10:30 p.m. Thu 6 p.m.–11 p.m. Fri–Sat 6 p.m.–12 a.m.	212-388-1990 www.backfortynyc. com	Burgers, ribs and fried chicken with waffles are the stars of the menu. Try the pecan fig pie. Oh my. It feels like a rustic old country farmhouse. $25 Sunday–Monday dinner specials.
Daily 11 a.m.–4 a.m.	212-688-9663 www.baker- streetnyc.com	A traditional Irish menu and bar. Good for watching rugby and soccer with real passionate fans. They offer many different specials during sporting events. $15 brunch on weekends includes two FREE drinks.

WHAT	DEAL	LOCATION
28 **Ballarò Caffé Prosciutteria** Italian Restaurant	6 p.m.–8 p.m. daily $6 wine FREE appetizers	77 Second Avenue (between 4th & 5th Streets) 2 Av (F) Astor Pl (4, 6, 6X) Bleecker St (4, 6, 6X) EAST VILLAGE
House-cured pork and beef		
29 **Bamboo 52** Sushi Restaurant & Bar	11 a.m.–9 p.m. Monday–Friday 2-for-1 beer, wine, well & cocktails Daily drink specials	344 West 52nd Street (between 8th & 9th Avenues) 50 St (A, C, E, 1, 2) 7 Av (B, D, E) HELL'S KITCHEN/ MIDTOWN WEST
Buy two sushi rolls get one free 12 a.m.–2 a.m. daily		
30 **Bar 515** Bar & Restaurant	5 p.m.–10 p.m. daily $3 Coors drafts $4 domestic drafts $5 specialty cocktails	515 Third Avenue (between 34th & 35th Streets) 33 St (4, 6, 6X) Grand Central–42 St (4, 5, 6, 6X, 7, 7X) MIDTOWN EAST
Twelve foot projector screen, DJ Thursday–Saturday		

MONICA DiNATALE

HOURS	CONTACT	365 EXTRAS
Daily 8 a.m.–12 a.m.	212-228-2969 www.ballaronyc.com	I start smiling as soon as I enter this brick and wine bottle lined bar. They have an endless selection of paninis. I like the della nonna with meatballs. Try the burrata or any one of their cheeses.
Mon–Tue 11 a.m.–2 a.m. Wed–Fri 11 a.m.–4 a.m. Sat 4 p.m.–4 a.m. Sun 4 p.m.–2 a.m.	212-315-2777 www.bamboo52nyc.com	Very good sushi and sashimi. I like the fantasy roll with banana, shrimp tempura and spicy tuna. Very sexy orange décor with a loungey bar area perfect for meeting friends.
Mon–Fri 5 p.m.–4 a.m. Sat–Sun 4 p.m.–4 a.m.	212-532-3300	A somewhat upscale take on a sports bar with twenty HD TVs. The burgers are huge and they offer nice sharing items like buffalo chicken sliders and pizzas. Try the 515 sangria.

	WHAT	DEAL	LOCATION
31	**Bar Coastal** Bar	4 p.m.–7 p.m. Monday–Friday $3 Bud & Bud Light drafts $3 well	1495 First Avenue (at 78th Street) 77 St (4, 6, 6X) UPPER EAST SIDE
	Buffet specials during sporting events		
32	**Bar Nine** Bar	3 p.m.–7 p.m. Monday–Friday $4 Bud Light bottles $6 margaritas & drafts $12 pitchers	807 Ninth Avenue (between 53rd & 54th Streets) 50 St (A, C, E, 1, 2) 59 St–Columbus Circle (1, 2, A, B, C, D) HELL'S KITCHEN/ MIDTOWN WEST
	Live music, DJ, dancing, karaoke		
33	**BarBossa** Brazilian Restaurant	Until 7 p.m. Monday–Friday $4 drafts $5 sangria & margaritas	232 Elizabeth Street (between East Houston & Prince Streets) Spring St (4, 6, 6X) Bowery (J) Broadway–Lafayette St (B, D, F, M) LITTLE ITALY
	Soccer bar, good for dates		

HOURS	CONTACT	365 EXTRAS
Mon–Sat 11 a.m.–4 a.m. Sun 12 p.m.–4 a.m.	212-288-6635 www.barcoastal.com	If you miss the beach you'll love their surf board covered walls and palm trees. Go for the atomic wings! Stay for the ½ lb. burgers. Lots of sauces, sides and large bar menu.
Daily 12 p.m.–4 a.m.	212-BAR-NINE www.barninenewyorkcity.com	This place can become a habit! It's perfect for catching live music. Plenty of seating up front and comfy couches in the back. On any night the front room can become a dance floor. Check the website for schedules.
Mon–Wed, Sun 11 a.m.– 11:30 p.m. Thu–Sat 11 a.m.– 12:30 a.m.	212-625-2340	I enjoyed the mussels in a coconut and cilantro broth. It's a small place that reminds me of an old fashioned diner. Great for an intimate dinner. Yummy capirinhas and mojitos.

	WHAT	DEAL	LOCATION
34	**Barbounia** Mediterranean Restaurant & Bar	3 p.m.–7 p.m. Monday–Friday ½ price drinks $21.95 2 ft. pizza of the day	250 Park Avenue South **(at 20th Street)** **23 St (4, 6, 6X, N, R)** **14 St–Union Sq** **(N, Q, R)** FLATIRON/ GRAMERCY
	$18.95 unlimited champagne brunch on weekends		
35	**Barcelona Bar** Bar	4 p.m.–7 p.m. Monday–Friday $3 Bud Light $4 domestic bottles & well	923 Eighth Avenue **(between 54th & 55th Streets)** **57 St–7 Av (N, Q, R)** **7 Av (B, D, E)** **50 St (A, C, E)** HELL'S KITCHEN/ MIDTOWN WEST
	One hundred plus shots		
36	**Barfly** Bar & Grill	Daily $4–$6 drinks 11 a.m.–8 p.m. Monday–Friday $2–$4 draft Bud & Miller Lite $3 other drafts & bottles $4 wine	244 Third Avenue **(at 20th Street)** **23 St (4, 6, 6X)** **3 Av (L)** **14 St–Union Sq (4, 5, 6, 6X)** FLATIRON/ GRAMERCY
	HD TVs, pool table, darts, sports specials		

24

HOURS	CONTACT	365 EXTRAS
Mon–Wed 11:30 a.m.– 11 p.m. Thu 11:30 a.m.– 11:30 p.m. Fri 11:30 a.m.– 12 a.m. Sat 10 a.m.– 12 a.m. Sun 10 a.m.– 10:30 p.m.	212-995-0242 www.barbounia.com	The modern terra cotta décor will take your breath away. Delicious hummus and tzatziki. Definitely an upscale version of traditional dishes. They attract a nice after work crowd. $24 three-course lunch on weekdays.
Mon–Sat 4 p.m.–4 a.m. Sun 4 p.m.–12 a.m.	212-245-3212 www.barcelona-barnyc.com	If you're looking for an extensive shot list, this is the place, some of which come with a costume. Give it a try! It's a narrow bar, great for drinks or catching a game. Just look for the blue shot glass in the window.
Mon–Sat 11 a.m.–4 a.m. Sun 12 p.m.–4 a.m.	212-473-9660 www.barflyny.com	They always offer great prices. A very comfortable bar with plenty of booths and solid bar food. Good for sports and lazy days. No pretenses here.

WHAT	DEAL	LOCATION
37 Barramundi Restaurant & Bar	Daily $4 bottles 6 p.m.–8 p.m. daily 2-for-1 drafts, well, sangria	67 Clinton Street (between Stanton & Rivington Streets) Essex St (J, M, Z) Delancey St (F) 2 Av (F) LOWER EAST SIDE
Try the nachos with homemade chips.		
38 Barrow Street Ale House Restaurant & Bar	11 a.m.–7 p.m. & 12 a.m.–4 a.m. Monday–Friday $3.50 drafts Sunday all day $3.50 drafts Monday $.40 wings, $3.50 drafts	15 Barrow Street (between 7th Avenue & 4th Street) Christopher St–Sheridan Sq (1, 2) W 4 St (A, B, C, D, E, F, M) Houston St (1, 2) THE VILLAGE
Pool table, darts, video games		
39 Bayard's Ale House Bar	3 p.m.–7 p.m. Monday–Friday $5 beer, wine & well Monday $.50 wings	533 Hudson Street (between 10th & Charles Streets) Christopher St–Sheridan Sq (1, 2) W 4 St (A, B, C, D, E, F, M) 14 St (1, 2, 3) THE VILLAGE
Early dinner specials Monday–Friday 4 p.m.–6:30 p.m.		

26

HOURS	CONTACT	365 EXTRAS
Daily 6 p.m.–4 a.m.	212-529-6999 www.barramundiny.com	The sangria is a treat! It's antique feel and large comfortable booths make this place warm and inviting. If you're meeting friends, plan to stay the night.
Sun–Thu 11 a.m.–2 a.m. Fri–Sat 11 a.m.–3 a.m.	212-691-6127 www.barrowstree-talehouse.com	This historic landmark pub dates back to 1897 and is the perfect place to grab a pint. They have twenty TVs, a bar food menu and a second bar downstairs. You'll feel like your part of history.
Mon–Fri 11:30 a.m.–4 a.m. Sat–Sun 11 a.m.–4 a.m.	212-989-0313	I am instantly transported to London or Ireland at this cute pub with twelve beers on tap. Try the shepherd's pie or a burger. They decorate for every holiday, are low key and full of locals.

WHAT	DEAL	LOCATION
40 **Beckett's** Bar & Grill	4 p.m.–8 p.m. Monday–Friday $5 Bud Light drafts & Stella $6 well	81 Pearl Street (between Coenties Alley & Hanover Square) Whitehall St (N, R) Broad St (J, Z) Wall St (2, 3) FINANCIAL DISTRICT
Sports bar, food and drink specials		
41 **Belmont Lounge** Bar & Restaurant	4 p.m.–7 p.m. daily $4 beer & well $5 wine, sangria & margaritas	117 East 15th Street (between Irving Place & Union Square East) 14 St–Union Sq (4, 5, 6, 6X, L, N, Q, R) UNION SQUARE
Private parties up to two hundred fifty people		
42 **Betel** Asian Restaurant	5 p.m.–7 p.m. Monday–Friday ½ price beer & wine	51 Grove Street (between Bleecker & West 4th Streets) Christopher St–Sheridan Sq (1, 2) W 4 St (A, B, C, D, E, F, M) Houston St (1, 2) THE VILLAGE
Seasonal drink specials, small plates menu		

HOURS	CONTACT	365 EXTRAS
Mon–Wed 11 a.m.–2 a.m. Thu–Sat 11 a.m.–3 a.m. Sun 11 a.m.–1 a.m.	212-269-1001 www.beckettsnyc.com	They offer a large outdoor seating area on a lovely, pedestrian-only cobblestone street. The menu includes everything from traditional Irish fare to lobster. Large portions and delicious burgers.
Daily 4 p.m.–4 a.m.	212-533-0009 www.belmontlounge-enyc.com	Cool red velvet curtains and exposed brick walls. Nice tapas menu and lounge seating. Order the Mediterranean plate to share. DJs on weekends take over the lounge for dancing. Right off Union Square.
Mon–Thu, Sun 6 p.m.–12 a.m. Fri–Sat 6 p.m.–1 a.m.	212-352-0460 www.betelnyc.com	They have a creative cocktail menu and I love the jalapeno tequila. The menu is an upscale take on Thai, Vietnamese food. Ordering small plates to share is a good way to go. Nice for a date.

WHAT	DEAL	LOCATION
43 **Blaggard's Pub & Restaurant** Irish Pub	4 p.m.–7 p.m. Mon–Sat; Mon: $4 beer, martinis, ½ price wings; Tue: $4 beer, ½ price wings; Wed: ½ price for ladies; Thu: $4 beer, $5 well & wine, ½ price potato skins; Fri: $4 beer, shots, ½ price wings; Sat: $4 drafts, ½ price apps	8 West 38th Street (between 5th & 6th Avenues) 42 St–Bryant Pk (B, D, F, M); Grand Central (4, 5, 6, 7); 34 St–Herald Sq (B, D, F, M, N, R) **MADISON SQUARE GARDEN/ PENN STATION**
Drink specials, sports specials, live music		
44 **Blarney Cove** Bar	Daily $3.50 pints	510 East 14th Street (between Avenue A & Avenue B) 1 Av (L) 3 Av (L) **EAST VILLAGE**
Jukebox, $.25 peanut machine		
45 **Blarney Rock Pub** Irish Pub	Daily $4 domestic bottles $5 imported bottles $6 drafts	137 West 33rd Street (between 6th & 7th Avenues) 34 St–Herald Sq (B, D, F, M, N, Q, R) 34 St–Penn Station (A, C, E, 1, 2, 3) **MADISON SQUARE GARDEN/ PENN STATION**
30 Affordable burgers and sandwiches near Penn Station		

HOURS	CONTACT	365 EXTRAS
Mon–Tue 11 a.m.–2 a.m. Wed 11 a.m.–3 a.m. Thu–Sat 11 a.m.–4 a.m. Sun 11 a.m.–10 p.m.	212-382-2611 www.blaggardspub-ny.com	Classic Irish pub with plenty of bar space and tables. Arrive before 10 p.m. to avoid a cover charge. They always have sports specials because they are close to the Garden.
Mon–Sat 8 a.m.–4 a.m. Sun 12 p.m.–4 a.m.	212-472-9284	An Irish dive bar with cheap drinks every day. You'll always find regulars sitting at the bar and the jukebox playing good ol' rock n' roll. No attitudes please.
Daily 8 a.m.–4 a.m.	212-947-0825 www.blarneyrock-pub.com	Good for a beer that doesn't break the bank. Fifteen beers on tap and good bar food. They have lots of food specials during sporting events. I prefer sitting upstairs on the patio and watching the crowds go by.

WHAT	DEAL	LOCATION
46 **Blarney Stone** Pub & Restaurant	Daily $4 drafts $5 well $11 pitchers	410 Eighth Avenue (between 29th & 30th Streets) 34 St–Penn Station (A, C, E, 1, 2, 3) 28 St (1, 2) MADISON SQUARE GARDEN/ PENN STATION
Arrive before 4 p.m. to save $1 on all drinks, $6 lunch special until 3 p.m.		
47 **Bleecker Street Bar** Bar	12 p.m.–8 p.m. daily $4.50 Bud, Bud Lite or Yuengling $5 well	56–58 Bleecker Street (between Lafayette & Crosby Streets) Bleecker St (4, 6, 6X) Broadway–Lafayette St (B, D, F, M) Prince St (N, R) NOHO
Darts, video games, pool table		
48 **Blind Pig** Bar & Restaurant	12 p.m.–8 p.m. Monday–Friday $2 off drafts $5 wine & well	233 East 14th Street (between 2nd & 3rd Avenues) 3 Av (L) 1 Av (L) 14 St–Union Sq (4, 5, 6, 6X) UNION SQUARE
Nine TVs, sports specials, outdoor seating		

MONICA DiNATALE

HOURS	CONTACT	365 EXTRAS
Mon–Sat 11 a.m.–4 a.m. Sun 12 p.m.–3 a.m.	212-594-5100	They are home to the New York City Social Sports Club so you will often find teams celebrating, win or loose! The upstairs bar is perfect for getting a little space. If you are stuck at Penn Station, give this place a try.
Daily 12 p.m.–4 a.m.	212-334-0244 www.bleeckerstreet-barnyc.com	This sports bar is roomy and comfortable with plenty of TVs. It's a great place to have a few drinks and catch a few innings. You can order food for delivery then try the photo booth to remember your evening.
Daily 11 a.m.–4 a.m.	212-209-1573 www.blindpigbar.com	Wings and boneless wings are offered with a variety of sauces like bad breath garlic butter. Yum! I am a fan of burgers served on english muffins. Good drinks, good food, good times.

WHAT	DEAL	LOCATION
49 **Blind Tiger Ale House** Bar & Restaurant	11:30 a.m.– 8 p.m. Monday–Friday $1 off drafts, cask beer, wine & prosecco FREE Murray's Cheese & baguettes 6 p.m. every Wednesday	**281 Bleecker Street** (at Jones Street) Christopher St–Sheridan Sq (1, 2) W 4 St (A, B, C, D, E, F, M) Houston St (1, 2) **THE VILLAGE**
Hosts breweries for special events, brunch daily		
50 **Blondie's** Sports Bar & Restaurant	4 p.m.–7 p.m. Monday–Friday Buy-1-get-1-FREE drinks	**212 West 79th Street** (between Amsterdam & Broadway) 79 St (1, 2) 72 St (1, 2, 3) 81 St–Museum of Natural History (A, B, C) **UPPER WEST SIDE**
HD TVs and a projector screen, back room for parties, sports specials		
51 **BLT Fish** Seafood Restaurant & Bar	5 p.m.–7 p.m. Monday–Friday $1 oyster & clams $5 drafts $6 cocktails	**21 West 17th Street** (between 5th & 6th Avenues) 6 Av (L) 14 St–Union Sq (F, M, N, Q, R) **UNION SQUARE**
Private parties, cooking classes, great raw bar		

MONICA DiNATALE

HOURS	CONTACT	365 EXTRAS
Daily 11:30 a.m.– 4 a.m.	212-462-4682 www.blindtigerale-house.com	A comfortabe classic beer bar with a relaxed vibe. Thirty craft beers on tap, including cask, and bartenders that know the difference. Good veal, lamb and meatball sliders.
Sun–Tue 11:30 a.m.– 12 a.m. Wed 11:30 a.m.– 1 a.m. Thu 11:30 a.m.– 2 a.m. Fri–Sat 11:30 a.m.– 3 a.m.	212-362-4360 www.blondiessports. com	The perfect sports bar with three huge seating areas. They handle large groups very well but definitely make a reservation for major sporting events. I am addicted to the toasted sesame grilled chicken tenders.
Mon–Wed 5:30 p.m.– 10 p.m. Thu 5:30 p.m.– 11 p.m. Fri–Sat 5:30 p.m. –11:30 p.m. Sun 5 p.m.– 10 p.m. Fish Shack on first floor only	212-691-8888 www.bltfish.com	Absolutely beautiful dining room with an upscale menu that includes $30–$50 entrees. It makes the bar deals even better! It's a nice choice for special occasions. The seafood is top notch.

	WHAT	DEAL	LOCATION
52	**Bocca** Italian Restaurant & Bar	5 p.m.– 7:30 p.m. daily $5 beer $7–$8 wine $8 well	39 East 19th Street (between Broadway & Park Avenue South) 23 St (4, 6, 6X, N, R) 14 St–Union Sq (N, Q, R) FLATIRON/ GRAMERCY
	Wine events, good for a date		
53	**Boss Tweeds Saloon** Bar & Restaurant	12 p.m.–8 p.m. daily $3 drafts & well $5 well $12 pitchers	115 Essex Street (between Delancey & Rivington Streets) Delancey St (F) Essex St (J, M, Z) 2 Av (F) LOWER EAST SIDE
	Year-round outdoor beer garden, FREE drinks on your birthday		
54	**Botanica Bar** Bar	Until 8 p.m. daily $1 off wine $3 well $4 drafts	47 East Houston Street (between Mulberry and Green Streets) Bleecker St (4, 6, 6X) Broadway–Lafayette St (B, D, F, M) Prince St (N, R) LITTLE ITALY
	Free karaoke, private parties, comedy shows		

HOURS	CONTACT	365 EXTRAS
Mon–Thu 12 p.m.–11 p.m. Fri–Sat 5:30 p.m.– 11:30 p.m. Sun 5:30 p.m.– 10:30 p.m.	212-387-1200 www.boccanyc.com	You must try one of the homemade pastas. I like the ox-tail ravioli in truffle brown butter. Authentic Italian food in a small romantic setting.
Daily 12 p.m.–4 a.m.	212-475-9997 www.bosstweeds.com	Super low key with tons of space. Beer pong, karaoke, DJs, skee ball and lots of drink specials. It's a dive bar that is clean and friendly. I am a sucker for beer gardens.
Mon–Fri 5 p.m.–4 a.m. Sat–Sun 6 p.m.–4 a.m.	212-343-7251	It's a tucked away dive bar with cool people and reasonable drinks. Nothing fancy or "trendy" here. The bartenders like to experiment with mixed drinks. Try something new and settle in for the evening.

WHAT	DEAL	LOCATION
55 **Bourbon Street Bar & Grille** New Orleans Restaurant & Bar	Daily $5 Hurricanes 11 a.m.–8 p.m. Mon–Fri: $1 off beer Mon: 2-for-1 Stella drafts; Tue: 2-for-1 Abita drafts; Wed: $5 Cajun specials, 2-for-1 Bud; Thu: 2-for-1 draft; Fri: $10 flights	346 West 46th Street (between 8th & 9th Avenues) 42 St–Port Authority Bus Terminal (A, C, E) 50 St (A, C, E) 49 St (N, Q, R) HELL'S KITCHEN/ MIDTOWN WEST
Live music, sports specials		
56 **Boxcar Lounge** Bar	6 p.m.–10 p.m. Monday– Thursday, 4 p.m.–8 p.m. Friday– Sunday Buy-1-get-1-FREE per person	168 Avenue B (between 10th & 11th Streets) 1 Av (L) EAST VILLAGE
Outdoor garden in the back, private parties		
57 **Brandy's Piano Bar** Bar & Live Music	4–8 p.m. daily $1 off all drinks	235 East 84th Street (between 2nd & 3rd Avenues) 86 St (4, 5, 6, 6X) 77 St (4, 6, 6X) UPPER EAST SIDE
Live music seven days a week, no cover		

MONICA DiNATALE

HOURS	CONTACT	365 EXTRAS
Daily 11 a.m.–4 a.m.	212-245-2030 www.bourbonny. com	The menu is gigantic and offers New Orleans classics like crawfish étouffée and po'boys. Fun vibe and jazz music, with unlimited mimosas and Bloody Marys at brunch.
Mon–Thu 6 p.m.–4 a.m. Fri–Sun 4 p.m.–4 a.m.	212-473-2830 www.boxcarlounge. com	The outdoor garden is heated. Good Bloody Marys and sangria. Bring in your brunch on the weekends and leave the drinks to them. The Christmas lights make me feel at home.
Daily 4 p.m.–4 a.m.	212-744-4949 www.brandyspiano- bar.com	This is a unique piano bar where most of the waitstaff are singers and maybe tomorrow's stars. You'll hear everything from The Beatles to Lady Gaga. Great energy and FREE entertainment!

WHAT	DEAL	LOCATION
58 **Brinkley's Broome Street** Pub & Restaurant	4 p.m.–7 p.m. Monday–Friday $6 well, wine & beer	406 Broome Street (between Lafayette & Cleveland Place) Spring St (4, 6, 6X) Canal St (4, 6, 6X) Bowery (J) LITTLE ITALY
Bloody Mary menu at brunch, $15 burger and beer special daily after 10:30 p.m.		
59 **Broadway Dive** Bar	4 p.m.–7 p.m. daily $2 off drafts $5 well & wine	2662 Broadway (at 101st Street) 96 St (1, 2, 3) 103 St (A, B, C, 1) UPPER WEST SIDE
Ongoing beer specials and seasonal tastings		
60 **Brother Jimmy's BBQ** Barbecue Restaurant & Bar (5 locations)	4 p.m.–7 p.m. Monday–Friday, Tuesdays all night ½ price appetizers 4 p.m.–7 p.m. Monday–Friday $2 Budweiser & frozen margaritas $3 well	428 Amsterdam Avenue (between 80th & 81st Streets) 79 St (1, 2) 86 St (1, 2) 81 St–Museum of Natural History (A,B,C) UPPER WEST SIDE
Get the bucket o'tips or the wings appetizers.		

HOURS	CONTACT	365 EXTRAS
Mon–Fri 11:30 a.m.– 2 a.m. Sat–Sun 11 a.m.–2 a.m.	212-680-5600 www.brinkleyspubs.com	This gastropub has an interesting menu with truffled mac and cheese and duck-fat fries. You can always find a seat at the large bar and they have a nice selection of craft beers on tap. Good place to rest after shopping in Soho.
Daily 12 p.m.–4 a.m.	212-865-2662 www.divebarnyc.com	This small bar has an eclectic selection of drafts and offers bottled beers to go. It's a dive bar that is scuba themed and filled with locals. Relax the day away.
Sun–Thu 4 p.m.–2 a.m. Fri–Sun 12 p.m.–2 a.m	212-501-7515 www.brotherjimmys.com	Any of these locations are great for barbecue in a lively atmosphere. The menu includes ribs, burgers and even salads. I like to order a bunch of appetizers for dinner. Fun for every occasion.

WHAT	DEAL	LOCATION
Brother Jimmy's BBQ Barbecue Restaurant & Bar (5 locations)	4 p.m.–7 p.m. Monday–Friday $3 Budweiser & Bud Light	181 Lexington Avenue (at 31st Street) 33 St (4, 6, 6X) 28 St (4, 6, 6X, N, R) MURRAY HILL
Get the bucket o'tips or the wings appetizers.		
Brother Jimmy's BBQ Barbecue Restaurant & Bar (5 locations)	3 p.m.–8 p.m. Monday–Friday, Tuesdays all night $3 Budweiser & Bud Light $4.50 margaritas	116 East 16th Street (between Park Avenue South & Irving Place) 14 St–Union Sq (4, 5, 6, 6X, L, N, Q, R) UNION SQUARE
Brother Jimmy's BBQ Barbecue Restaurant & Bar (5 locations)	4 p.m.–7 p.m. Monday–Friday $3 mini-appetizers $3 well, drafts & margaritas	1485 Second Avenue (between 77th & 78th Streets) 77 St (4, 6, 6X) 86 St (4, 5, 6, 6X) UPPER EAST SIDE

MONICA DiNATALE

HOURS	CONTACT	365 EXTRAS
Sun–Thu 4 p.m.–2 a.m. Fri–Sun 12 p.m.–2 a.m	212-779-7427 www.brotherjimmys.com	Any of these locations are great for barbecue in a lively atmosphere. The menu includes ribs, burgers and even salads. I like to order a bunch of appetizers for dinner. Fun for every occasion.
Sun–Thu 4 p.m.–2 a.m. Fri–Sun 12 p.m.–2 a.m	212-673-6465 www.brotherjimmys.com	
Sun–Thu 4 p.m.–2 a.m. Fri–Sun 12 p.m.–2 a.m	212-288-0999 www.brotherjimmys.com	

	WHAT	DEAL	LOCATION
60	**Brother Jimmy's BBQ** Barbecue Restaurant & Bar (5 locations)	Dinner specials only	416 Eighth Avenue (at 31st Street) 34 St–Penn Station (A, C, E, 1, 2, 3) 28 St (1, 2) MADISON SQUARE GARDEN/ PENN STATION
	Get the bucket o'tips or the wings appetizers.		
61	**Bull McCabe's/ Ryan's** Irish Pub	4 p.m.–8 p.m. daily $1 off bar	29 St. Mark's Place (between 2nd & 3rd Avenues) Astor Pl (4, 6, 6X) 8 St–Nyu (N, R) 3 Av (L) EAST VILLAGE
	Pool table, jukebox, darts		
62	**Bull's Head Tavern** Bar	1 p.m.–7 p.m. daily $3 drafts $4 "beer of the month" all day	295 Third Avenue (at 23rd Street) 23 St (4, 6, 6X, N, R) 28 St (4, 6, 6X) FLATIRON/ GRAMERCY
	Band on Fridays, DJ on Saturdays, pool tables, darts, video games		

HOURS	CONTACT	365 EXTRAS
Sun–Thu 4 p.m.–2 a.m. Fri–Sun 12 p.m.–2 a.m	212-967-7603 www.brotherjimmys.com	Any of these locations are great for barbecue in a lively atmosphere. The menu includes ribs, burgers and even salads. I like to order a bunch of appetizers for dinner. Fun for every occasion.
Daily 12 p.m.–4 a.m.	212-982-9895	Inexpensive food and drinks every day! They attract a crowd for the electronic dartboard. You must have an Irish car bomb to finish off your evening.
Daily 1 p.m.–4 a.m.	212-685-2589 www.welovebars.com/bullshead-tavern/	They keep things festive by decorating for every holiday. The beer selection makes it hard to pick just one and there are plenty of specials and games to keep you busy. Twenty beers on tap.

	WHAT	DEAL	LOCATION
63	**Burp Castle** Bar	4 p.m.–8 p.m. Monday–Friday $1 off draft beer	41 East Seventh Street (between 2nd Avenue & Taras Shevchenko Place) Astor Pl (4, 6, 6X) 8 St–Nyu (N, R) 3 Av (L) EAST VILLAGE
	FREE pommes frites Sundays, Mondays and Wednesdays 5 p.m.–6:30 p.m.		
64	**Café el Portal** Mexican Restaurant	4 p.m.–7 p.m. Monday–Friday $3.50 Mexican beers $6 margaritas $8 flavored margaritas	174 Elizabeth Street (between Spring & Kenmare Streets) Bowery (J) Spring St (4, 6, 6X) Grand St (B, D) LITTLE ITALY
	Extensive tequila and drink menu		
65	**Cake Shop** Bar & Live Music Venue	5 p.m.–8 p.m. daily 2-for-1 drinks	152 Ludlow Street (between Stanton & Rivington Streets) Delancey St (F) Essex St (J, M, Z) 2 Av (F) LOWER EAST SIDE
46	Check online schedule for live bands starting at 8 p.m. daily.		

HOURS	CONTACT	365 EXTRAS
Mon–Thu 5 p.m.–12 a.m. Fri 5 p.m.–2 a.m. Sat 4 p.m.–2 a.m. Sun 4 p.m.– 12 a.m.	212-982-4576 www.burpcastlenyc. wordpress.com	Twelve craft beers on tap. The pommes frites are addicting and they offer fifteen different sauces. Candlelit and low key with soft "monk like" music.
Mon–Sat 12 p.m.– 10:30 p.m.	212-226-4642 www.cafeelpor- talnyc.com	Don't let the basement entrance scare you away, this place is the real deal. Authentic Mexican food including my favorite, al pastor tacos. The margaritas are good, but try the micheladas.
Café hours 9 a.m.–2 a.m. daily **Bar hours** Sun–Thu 5 p.m.–2 a.m. Fri–Sat 5 p.m.–4 a.m.	212-253-0036 www.cake-shop.com	When you enter it looks like an eclectic coffee shop but they offer tons of live music downstairs. Some of it is FREE or they have reasonable covers. I really like it's unique atmosphere.

WHAT	DEAL	LOCATION
66 Calico Jack's Cantina Mexican Restaurant & Bar	6 p.m.–12 a.m. Monday–Wednesday Monday: $3 margaritas Tuesday: $1 beer Wednesday: $1 margaritas Monday–Wednesday ½ price drinks with $5 wristband	800 Second Avenue (between 42nd & 43rd Streets) Grand Central–42 St (4, 5, 6, 6X, 7, 7X, S) **GRAND CENTRAL**
Sports specials, drinking specials		
67 Cask Bar & Kitchen Bar & Restaurant	4 p.m.–8 p.m. Monday–Friday $5 drafts $6 wine $7 red and white sangria	167 East 33rd Street (between 3rd & Lexington Avenues) 33 St (4, 6, 6X) 28 St (4, 6, 6X) Grand Central–42 St (7, 7X) **MURRAY HILL**
Private party room downstairs, cask beers		
68 Cellar Bar Lounge	5 p.m.–8 p.m. Monday–Friday $10 specialty cocktails	40 West 40th Street (between Fifth & Sixth Avenues) 42 St-Bryant Pk (B, D, F, M) 5 Av (7, 7X) Times Sq-42 St (S) **MIDTOWN EAST**
Private parties, DJ schedule online		

HOURS	CONTACT	365 EXTRAS
Mon–Fri 11 a.m.–4 a.m. Sat–Sun 4 p.m.–4 a.m.	212-557-4300 www.calicojacksnyc.com	They are a good pit stop if you're going to Grand Central and in the mood to let loose after a tough day. There is usually a DJ and dancing. If you want to boogie, this place is for you.
Mon–Fri 4 p.m.–4 a.m. Sat–Sun 12 p.m.–4 a.m.	212-300-4924 www.casknyc.com	Cool lighting and blonde wood give them a chilled vibe. They have a good selection of craft beers and usually two cask choices. Try the sliders. I like the bar downstairs.
Mon 5 p.m.–12 a.m. Tue–Wed 5 p.m.–1 a.m. Thu 5 p.m.–2 a.m. Fri 5 p.m.–4 a.m. Sat 10 p.m.–4 a.m.	212-642-2211 www.cellarbarbry-antparkhotel.com	Dress to impress at this absolutely cavernous gothic lounge. They made atmosphere an art with wrought iron gates and beautiful archways. You'll save $5 per drink by getting there early! Beers are $8.

WHAT	DEAL	LOCATION
69 **Chelsea Bar & Grill** Restaurant & Bar	4 p.m.–7 p.m. Monday–Friday $4 beer, wine, well $6 appetizers like guacamole, mozzarella sticks, and popcorn shrimp	675 Ninth Avenue (between 46th & 47th Streets) 50 St (A, C, E) 42 St–Port Authority Bus Terminal (A, C, E) 49 St (N, Q, R) HELL'S KITCHEN/ MIDTOWN WEST
Pre/post theater menus, rotating taps		
70 **Churrascaria Plataforma** Brazilian Steakhouse & Bar	4 p.m.–6 p.m. Monday–Friday Buy-1-get-1-FREE drinks FREE bar snacks	316 West 49th Street (between 8th & 9th Avenues) 50 St (A, C, E, 1, 2) 49 St (N, Q, R) TIMES SQUARE/ THEATER DISTRICT
Good for special occasions, prix-fixe menus		
71 **Churrascaria Tribeca** Brazilian Steakhouse & Bar	4 p.m.–7 p.m. Monday–Friday Buy-1-get-1-FREE drinks FREE bar snacks	221 West Broadway (between White and Franklin Streets) Franklin St (1, 2) Canal St (A, C, E, N, R) TRIBECA
Private parties, live Brazilian music Fridays and Saturdays		

50

HOURS	CONTACT	365 EXTRAS
Daily 11:30 a.m.– 4 a.m.	212-974-9002	I am in love with their huge, delicious burgers and big portions in general. It's nice to sit up front when the windows are open in nice weather. Near the theatres yet an avenue away from the crowds.
Sun–Mon 12 p.m.–11 p.m. Tue–Sat 12 p.m.–12 a.m.	212-245-0505 www.churrasca-riaplataforma.com	The best Brazilian steakhouse in the city. The meat never stops coming! Everything is big including the dessert tray, so go here hungry. Try everything.
Mon 5 p.m.–11 p.m. Tue–Thu 5 p.m.–12 a.m. Fri–Sat 12 p.m.–12 a.m. Sun 12 p.m.–11 p.m.	212-925-6969 www.churrascariatri-beca.com	Another Brazilian steakhouse far from the hustle and bustle of Times Square. Bring your appetite and the whole family. This place is a blast with groups!

	WHAT	DEAL	LOCATION
72	**Cilantro** Mexican Restaurant (3 locations)	4 p.m.–7 p.m. Monday–Friday $5 margaritas & sangria $10 chicken, shrimp or vegetable fajitas, every Monday from 4 p.m. (cash only)	**485 Columbus Avenue** (at 83rd Street) 81 St–Museum of Natural History (A, B, C) 86 St (A, B, C, 1, 2) UPPER WEST SIDE
	Outdoor seating, weekend brunch		
72	**Cilantro** Mexican Restaurant (3 locations)	4 p.m.–7 p.m. Monday–Friday $5 margaritas & sangria $10 chicken, shrimp or vegetable fajitas, every Monday from 4 p.m. (cash only)	**1321 First Avenue** (at 71st Street) 77 St, 86 St (6) UPPER EAST SIDE
72	**Cilantro** Mexican Restaurant (3 locations)	4 p.m.–7 p.m. Monday–Friday $5 margaritas & sangria $10 chicken, shrimp or vegetable fajitas, every Monday from 4 p.m. (cash only)	**1712 Second Avenue** (at 89th Street) 77 St, 86 St (6) UPPER EAST SIDE

MONICA DiNATALE

HOURS	CONTACT	365 EXTRAS
Mon–Thu 12 p.m.–12 a.m. Fri 12 p.m.–1 a.m. Sat–Sun 11 a.m.–1 a.m.	212-712-9090 www.cilantronyc. com	Delicious freshly made guacamole and an authentic Mexican atmosphere make them a winner. I love the chicken quesadillas and the queso fundito. A great choice for Cinco de Mayo.
Mon–Thu 12 p.m.–12 a.m. Fri 12 p.m.–1 a.m. Sat–Sun 11 a.m.–1 a.m.	212-537-4040 www.cilantronyc. com	
Mon–Thu 12 p.m.–12 a.m. Fri 12 p.m.–1 a.m. Sat–Sun 11 a.m.–1 a.m.	212-722-4242 www.cilantronyc. com	

	WHAT	DEAL	LOCATION
73	**City Crab and Seafood Company** Seafood Restaurant	4 p.m.–7 p.m. daily, 12 p.m.–7 p.m. Sunday ½ price drinks & appetizers	235 Park Avenue South (at 19th Street) 23 St (4, 6, 6X) 14 St–Union Sq (4, 5, 6, 6X, N, Q, R) UNION SQUARE
	Weekend brunch, good raw bar and steam pots		
74	**Cleopatra's Needle** Mediterranean Restaurant & Live Jazz	4 p.m.– 7:30 p.m. daily ½ price martinis & wine Reduced prices on bar	2485 Broadway (between 92nd & 93rd Streets) 86 St (1, 2) 96 St (A, B, C, 1, 2, 3) UPPER WEST SIDE
	No cover live jazz with $10 minimum per person		
75	**Common Ground** Bar	4 p.m.–8 p.m. Monday–Friday $3 drafts, $4 well & wine, $5 specialty cocktails, Buy 2 get 1 FREE appetizers & sandwiches; 12 p.m.–7 p.m. Saturday & Sunday $3 drafts, $4 well, wine & Cajun Bloody Marys	206 Avenue A (between 12th & 13th Streets) 1 Av (L) 3 Av (L) EAST VILLAGE
54	Board games like Connect Four® and Scrabble®, trivia nights		

HOURS	CONTACT	365 EXTRAS
Mon–Thu, Sun 12 p.m.–11 p.m. Fri–Sat 12 p.m.–12 a.m.	212-529-3800 www.citycrabnyc.com	They have an enormous selection of fresh fish and a two level upscale dining room. Take advantage of the appetizer deals, they will fill you up. If you want to splurge, go for the Maine lobster.
Mon–Tue 3:30 p.m.–2 a.m. Wed–Thu 3:30 p.m.–3 a.m. Fri–Sat 3:30 p.m.–4 a.m. Sun 3 p.m.–2 a.m.	212-769-6969 www.cleopatras-needleny.com	Great Mediterranean food and live jazz with no cover charge. The music is always good and they have a nice martini list. The everything appetizer is great to share and includes hummus, falafel and stuffed grape leaves.
Mon–Thu 4 p.m.–2 a.m. Fri 4 p.m.–4 a.m. Sat 12 p.m.–4 a.m. Sun 12 p.m.–2 a.m.	212-228-6231 www.commongroundnyc.com	Open mic Sundays, trivia Wednesdays, and weekend brunch with unlimited Bloody Marys means there is always something of interest happening here. The vibe is grand and plush complete with crystal chandeliers.

WHAT	DEAL	LOCATION
76 Copia Bar & Restaurant	5:30 p.m.– 8 p.m. Monday–Friday ½ price cocktails ½ price appetizers $4 draft	307 East 53rd Street (between 1st & 2nd Avenues) Lexington Av/53 St (E, M) 51 St (4, 6, 6X) 59 St (4, 5, 6, 6X) MIDTOWN EAST
DJ Wednesday through Saturday nights		
77 Copper Door Tavern Bar & Restaurant	Daily $3 drafts $10 pitchers Drink & food specials	272 Third Avenue (between 22nd & 23rd Streets) 23 St (4, 6, 6X, N, R) 28 St (4, 6, 6X) FLATIRON/ GRAMERCY
Tuesdays 2-for-1 burgers, check website for specials		
78 Corner Bistro Bar & Burgers	Daily $3.00–$4.25 drafts $5.25 bottles $7.00 Guinness pub can	331 West 4th Street (at Jane & West 4th Streets) 8 Av (L) 14 St (A, C, E, 1, 2, 3) THE VILLAGE
They have one of the best burgers in the city for $6.75!		

MONICA DiNATALE

HOURS	CONTACT	365 EXTRAS
Tue 4 p.m.–2 a.m. Wed–Fri 4 p.m.–4 a.m. Sat 8 p.m.–4 a.m.	212-838-0007 www.copianyc.com	This place is a combination of a fancy restaurant, sports bar and club. Good flatbread pizzas and appetizer menu for sharing. Get there early to enjoy a quiet drink and the seared ahi tuna.
Mon 3 p.m.–12 a.m. Tue–Wed 3 p.m.–2 a.m. Thu 12 p.m.–3 a.m. Fri 10 a.m.–4 a.m. Sat 12 p.m.–4 a.m. Sun 12 p.m.–12 a.m.	212-254-3870 www.copperdoor-tavern.com	They offer so many specials, you have to save money! On Sundays take advantage of the $5 hangover breakfast; bacon, egg and cheese on an english muffin with tator tots.
Mon–Sat 11:30 a.m.– 4 a.m. Sun 12 p.m.–4 a.m.	212-242-9502 www.cornerbistrony.com	Classic popular burger joint. Old world bar feel with booths in the back. If there is a line, wait! Menu consists of burgers and grilled cheese. That's it. They are delicious!

WHAT	DEAL	LOCATION
79 **Cornerstone Tavern** Restaurant & Bar	11 a.m.–7 p.m. Monday–Friday $4 drafts & well	961 Second Avenue (between 50th & 51st Streets) Lexington Av/53 St (E, M) 51 St (4, 6, 6X) 5 Av/53 St (E, M) MIDTOWN EAST
Fourteen HD TVs, rotating taps, karaoke		
80 **Cowgirl Sea-Horse** Restaurant & Bar	4 p.m.–7 p.m. daily $4 drafts & wine	259 Front Street (between Peck Slip & Dover Street) Fulton St (2, 3) Chambers St (J, Z) Brooklyn Bridge–City Hall (4, 5, 6, 6X) SOUTH STREET SEAPORT
Seasonal food and drink specials		
81 **Coyote Ugly** Bar	4 p.m.–7 p.m. Monday–Friday 2-for-1 drinks 8 p.m.–12 a.m. Tuesdays $7 Bud & Bud Light pitchers	153 First Avenue (between 9th & 10th Streets) 1 Av (L) 3 Av (L) Astor Pl (4, 6, 6X) EAST VILLAGE
Beautiful bartenders and lively dancing		

HOURS	CONTACT	365 EXTRAS
Mon–Sat 11 a.m.–4 a.m. Sun 12 p.m.–4 a.m.	212-888-7403 www.cornerstone-tavern.com	You can't miss this huge "corner" sports bar with trivia, karaoke and lots of rotating specials. I like the $5 truffled popcorn. Brunch on weekends includes one FREE beverage for $11–$13.
Mon–Thu 11 a.m.–11 p.m. Fri 11 a.m.–12 a.m. Sat 10 a.m.–12 a.m. Sun 10 a.m.–11 p.m.	212-608-7873 www.cowgirl-seahorse.com	Keep walking until you see the highway! The menu is a cross between Tex-Mex and New Orleans fare. Try the shrimp stuffed jalapenos wrapped with bacon. The sweet potato fries sprinkled with pecans are heavenly.
Mon–Thu 2 p.m.–4 a.m. Fri–Sun 12:30 p.m.–4 a.m.	212-477-4431 www.coyoteuglysaloon.com	The rumors are true. Bartenders dance on the bar, pour shots, and are fun to watch. Participation is welcomed! It's a great time but can get crowded on weekends.

	WHAT	DEAL	LOCATION
82	**Crema** Mexican Restaurant	5 p.m.–7 p.m. Tuesday–Sunday 2-for-1 margaritas, sangria, Mexican beers & wine	111 West 17th Street (between 6th & 7th Avenues) 14 St (F, M) 18 St (1, 2) 6 Av (L) FLATIRON/ GRAMERCY
	Tequila tasting events, private parties		
83	**Crocodile Lounge** Bar	12 p.m.–7 p.m. daily $1 off drafts $3 Yuengling $4 well FREE pizza with drinks	325 East 14th Street (between 1st & 2nd Avenues) 3 Av (L) 1 Av (L) 14 St–Union Sq (4, 5, 6, 6X) EAST VILLAGE
	Sports bar, jukebox, skee ball		
84	**Croxley's** Ale House & Eatery	5 p.m.–7 p.m. Monday–Friday $1 off beer $5 beer of the week 4 p.m.–1 a.m. Saturday–Sunday $.10 boneless wings $.20 wings	28 Avenue B (between 2nd & 3rd Streets) 2 Av (F) Essex St (J, M, Z) Delancey St (F) EAST VILLAGE
	Lots of visting brewery specials and cask ales		

HOURS	CONTACT	365 EXTRAS
Mon 12 p.m.–10 p.m. Tue–Thu 12 p.m.–10:30 p.m. Fri 12 p.m.–11 p.m. Sat 11:30 a.m.–11 p.m. Sun 11:30 a.m.–10 p.m.	212-691-4477 www.cremarestaurante.com	Beautiful upscale Mexican menu with creative drinks like a spicy mango margarita. I like the carne asada tacos. $19.95 one hour unlimited mimosa brunch on weekends.
Daily 12 p.m.–4 a.m.	212-477-7747	You can't go wrong with free pizza! It's divey and does get crowded, so be prepared. It is still fun. You will leave with money in your pocket and a full belly.
Mon–Thu 5 p.m.–1 a.m. Fri 5 p.m.–2 a.m. Sat 12 p.m.–2 a.m. Sun 12 p.m.–1 a.m.	212-253-6140 www.croxley.com	You should stop here if you're a wings fan. They are delicious and a great deal! With thirty four beers on tap you can't get bored. I am a fan of their specials like cask tastings, saison week and craft beer takeovers.

	WHAT	DEAL	LOCATION
85	**Cucina Di Pesce** Italian Restaurant	4 p.m.–8 p.m. daily Buy-1-get-1-FREE drinks & appetizers FREE mussels marinara at bar	87 East 4th Street (between 2nd & 3rd Avenues) 2 Av (F) Bleecker St (4, 6, 6X) Astor Pl (4, 6, 6X) EAST VILLAGE
	Early-bird specials, homemade pasta		
86	**Daltons** Bar & Grill	12 p.m.–8 p.m. daily $4 drafts of beer of the month $4 bottles $5 well, wine, specialty martinis & shots	611 Ninth Avenue (between 43rd & 44th Streets) 42 St–Times Sq (1, 2, 3, 7, 7X, A, C, E, N, Q, R) TIMES SQUARE/ THEATER DISTRICT
	Beers of the month and shots are always $4–$5.		
87	**Darbar** Indian Restaurant	5 p.m.–8 p.m. daily $4 beer & wine $6 top-shelf liquor FREE appetizers	152 East 46th Street (between 3rd & Lexington Avenues) Grand Central–42 St (4, 5, 6, 6X, 7, 7X) 51 St (4, 6, 6X) GRAND CENTRAL
	Unlimited lunch buffet $12.95 from 11:30 a.m.–4 p.m. daily, lunch boxes to go $8–$9		

MONICA DiNATALE

HOURS	CONTACT	365 EXTRAS
Daily 2:30 p.m.– 12 a.m.	212-260-6800 www.cucinadipesce. com	Delicious Italian food with a focus on seafood. You can't argue with free mussels! Try the cioppino bursting with fresh fish. I would definitely plan a date, sit in the enclosed glass area and enjoy.
Mon–Fri 11 a.m.–4 a.m. Sat–Sun 10 a.m.–4 a.m.	212-245-5511 www.daltonsbarnyc. com	Huge Irish bar with fifteen TVs and twenty five beers on tap. Try the baby beet and goat cheese salad or the chicken panini. Close to Midtown and the Theater District.
Mon–Thu, Sun 11:30 a.m.– 10:30 p.m. Fri–Sat 11:30 a.m.– 11 p.m.	212-681-4500 www.darbarny.com	The appetizers at the bar are very satisfying. They offer an extensive menu with very good Indian food in an upscale bar and dining room. Stay for dinner and share the rosemary naan and chicken mango.

	WHAT	DEAL	LOCATION
88	**Dark Horse** Bar & Restaurant	4 p.m.–6 p.m. Monday–Friday $4 Coors pints $5 well $25 beer towers (8 Pints)	17 Murray Street (between Church Street & Broadway) **Chambers Street (A,C)** **City Hall (R,W)** **Park Place (2, 3)** TRIBECA
	Eighteen HD TVs, twenty four drafts		
89	**Dave's Tavern** Bar	Daily $4 beers 4 p.m.–7 p.m. daily $3–$5 beers $5 well & shots	574 Ninth Avenue, Suite 7 (between 41st & 42nd Streets) **Times Sq–42 St (1, 2, 3, 7, 7X, A, C, E, N, Q, R)** TIMES SQUARE/ THEATER DISTRICT
	Pool table, seven HD TVs, sports specials		
90	**d.b.a.** Bar	1 p.m.– 7:30 p.m. daily $5 drafts, wine & well	41 First Avenue (between 2nd & 3rd Streets) **1 Av (L)** **3 Av (L)** **14 St–Union Sq (4, 5, 6, 6X)** EAST VILLAGE
64	FREE bagels and lox Sundays, craft beers and special tastings		

HOURS	CONTACT	365 EXTRAS
Mon–Thu 11 a.m.–1 a.m. Sat–Sun 11 a.m.–2 a.m.	212-608-3900 www.darkhorseny.com	Try the homemade potato chips and the Jameson chipotle wings. The wings come in ten flavors so order a few to pick your favorite. The menu is huge and includes pastas, steaks and Irish favorites.
Mon–Sat 11 a.m.–4 a.m. Sun 11:30 a.m.–4 a.m.	212-244-4408 www.davestavernnyc.com	This is a classic dive bar with a friendly atmosphere and FREE nuts at the bar. They attract sports fans and locals looking for a deal. Good place to grab a quick drink near Port Authority.
Daily 1 p.m.–4 a.m.	212-475-5097 www.drinkgoodstuff.com	A beer lover's paradise. They have fifteen beers on tap and a cask ale selection. More importantly, they are just plain cool. They also have a large selection of twenty plus whiskeys. Sister bar to d.b.a in New Orleans.

WHAT	DEAL	LOCATION
91 **Dempsey's** Pub & Restaurant	4 p.m.– 7:45 p.m. daily Buy-1-get-1-FREE drinks FREE fries with 2nd round $15 for bucket (5) $20 with wings	61 Second Avenue **(between 3rd & 4th Streets)** **2 Av (F)** **Bleecker St (4, 6, 6X)** **Astor Pl (4, 6, 6X)** EAST VILLAGE
HD TVs, sports specials, pool table, darts, live music, nightly specials		
92 **Dewey's Flatiron** Bar & Restaurant	4:30 p.m.– 7 p.m. Monday–Friday $4 Bud Light drafts & Coronas $5 well & margaritas	210 Fifth Avenue **(at 26th Street)** **28 St (N, R)** **23 St (F, M, N, R)** FLATIRON/ GRAMERCY
Seventeen HD TVs, sports specials, private rooms		
93 **Dinosaur Bar-B-Que** Barbecue Restaurant	3 p.m.–7 p.m. Monday–Friday $1 off beer, wine & well	700 West 125th Street **(between 12st Street & Riverside Drive)** **125 St (1)** **137 St–City College (1)** HARLEM
Live music		

MONICA DINATALE

HOURS	CONTACT	365 EXTRAS
Daily 12 p.m.–4 a.m.	212-388-0662 www.dempseyspub.com	Nice upscale Irish pub. Get the sweet potato fries. It's the kind of place where you can spend an afternoon in the blink of an eye. Anything fried is huge and tasty. Outdoor seating.
Mon–Thu 11:30 a.m.– 12 a.m. Fri 11:30 a.m.– 2 a.m. Sat 11:30 a.m.– 3 a.m. Sun 11:30 a.m.– 9 p.m.	212-696-BEER www.deweysflatiron.com	San Diego Chargers bar during football season. They carry all sports with twenty four beers on tap and can host large private parties. It's that comfortable neighborhood bar you like to visit.
Mon–Thu 11:30 a.m.– 11 p.m. Fri–Sat 11:30 a.m.– 12 a.m. Sun 12 p.m.– 10 p.m.	212-694-1777 www.dinosaurbarbeque.com	The authentic St. Louis cut ribs are scrumptious. This is the real deal. It has a huge bar and dining area making it perfect for groups of any size. If feeling adventurous, ride your bike to the end of the Riverside Park bike path.

	WHAT	DEAL	LOCATION
94	**Disiac Lounge** Bar & Lounge	4 p.m.–8 p.m. daily ½ off second round	402 West 54th Street (between 9th & 10th Avenues) 50 St (A, C, E, 1, 2) 59 St–Columbus Circle (1, 2, A, B, C, D) HELL'S KITCHEN/ MIDTOWN WEST
	Daily drink specials		
95	**Dive 75** Bar	5 p.m.–7 p.m. Monday– Thursday, 4 p.m.–7 p.m. Friday $2 off draft beers $5 well & wine	101 West 75th Street (at Columbus Avenue) 72 St (A, B, C, 1, 2, 3) 81 St–Museum of Natural History (A, B, C) UPPER WEST SIDE
	Ongoing beer specials and seasonal tastings		
96	**Dive Bar** Bar & Restaurant	4 p.m.–7 p.m. Monday–Friday $2 off drafts $5 well & wine	732 Amsterdam Avenue (between 95th & 96th Streets) 96 St (A, B, C, 1, 2, 3) 103 St (1) UPPER WEST SIDE
	Brewery tastings, live music		

68

HOURS	CONTACT	365 EXTRAS
Mon–Tue 5 p.m.–1:30 a.m. Wed 5 p.m.–2 a.m. Thu–Fri 5 p.m.–4 a.m. Sat 6 p.m.–4 a.m.	212-586-9880 www.disiacloung-enyc.com	Intimate, cool and colorful with a nice outdoor garden in the back. Great martini list, excellent sangria, and light eats like paninis and salads. A nice 'find' in the neighborhood on a quiet street.
Mon–Thu 5 p.m.–2 a.m. Fri 3 p.m.–4 a.m. Sat 12 p.m.–4 a.m. Sun 12 p.m.–2 a.m.	212-362-7518 www.divebarnyc. com	Not a dive bar, just scuba-themed. A relaxing place to play board games and chill all day. There is a nice amount of bar seating and FREE candy at the bar.
Daily 11:30 a.m.– 4 a.m.	212-749-4358 www.divebarnyc. com	A favorite! Great scuba themed neighborhood bar. Amazing homemade sweet potato chips with cayenne pepper. They always have visiting breweries and interesting events. You will leave wanting more.

WHAT	DEAL	LOCATION
97 Do Hwa Korean Restaurant & Bar	5 p.m.– 7:30 p.m. Monday–Friday ½ off cocktails $5 well & wine $7 martinis	55 Carmine Street (between Bedford & 7th Avenue) Houston St (1, 2) Christopher St–Sheridan Sq (1, 2) Spring St (A, C, E) THE VILLAGE
Dinner and holiday specials		
98 Doc Watson's Pub & Restaurant	11 a.m.–7 p.m. daily $2.50 domestic bottles $3 pints of Bud, Bud Light, Harp & Yuengling $10 for 1 beer & 1 appetizer	1490 Second Avenue (between 77th & 78th Streets) 77 St (4, 6, 6X) 86 St (4, 5, 6, 6X) UPPER EAST SIDE
$13.95 brunch includes two FREE drinks on Saturdays and Sundays.		
99 Docks Oyster Bar Seafood Restaurant	3 p.m.–7 p.m. Monday–Friday ½ price drafts $.50 clams $1 oysters $5 well $6 wine $3–$6 appetizers	633 Third Avenue (between 40th & 41st Streets) Grand Central–42 St (4, 5, 6, 6X, 7, 7X, S) MURRAY HILL
$25 bottomless weekend brunch 11:30 a.m.– 3 p.m., prix-fixe lunch and dinner menus		

MONICA DINATALE

HOURS	CONTACT	365 EXTRAS
Mon 4 p.m.–10 p.m. Tue–Wed 11:30 a.m.– 10 p.m. Thu 11:30 a.m.– 11 p.m. Fri 11:30 a.m.– 12 a.m. Sat 3 p.m.–12a.m. Sun 3 p.m.–10p.m.	212-414-1224 www.dohwanyc.com	They take authentic Korean food and make it sexy in a modern Village space. The menu for four is $29 per person for dinner and a great way to sample many dishes.
Daily 11 a.m.–4 a.m.	212-988-5300 www.docwatsons.com	Great Irish Pub and sports bar that offers live music and a beer garden in the back. They book traditional Irish bands. Very tasty half-pound burgers and bar munchies. Definitely have a Guinness.
Daily 11:30 a.m.– 11 p.m.	212-986-8080 www.docksoyster-bar.com	It's a special occasion restaurant that gets a great bar crowd after work. Everybody comes for the deals on oysters and clams. Feel classy and save money at the same time.

	WHAT	DEAL	LOCATION
100	**Down The Hatch** Sports Bar	12 p.m.–8 p.m. Monday–Friday ½ price bar Daily drink specials that rotate	179 West 4th Street (between 6th & 7th Avenues) W 4 St (A, B, C, D, E, F, M) Christopher St–Sheridan Sq (1, 2) Houston St (1, 2) THE VILLAGE
	Atomic wings, nine HD TVs, beer pong, foosball		
101	**Dublin 6** Pub & Restaurant	4 p.m.–7 p.m. Monday–Friday $4 bottled beer $4–$5 drafts	575 Hudson Street (between 11th & Bank Streets) Christopher St–Sheridan Sq (1, 2) 8 Av (L) 14 St (1, 2, 3) THE VILLAGE
	Sporting events including soccer, outdoor seating		
102	**Duke's** Barbecue Restaurant (2 locations)	4 p.m.–7 p.m. Monday–Friday ½ price drafts, bottles, specialty cocktails	99 East 19th Street (at Park Avenue South) 23 St (4, 6, 6X) 14 St–Union Sq (N, Q, R, 4, 5, 6, 7, 7X) FLATIRON/ GRAMERCY
	Sports specials, trivia nights, beer pong		

MONICA DiNATALE

HOURS	CONTACT	365 EXTRAS
Daily 12 p.m.–4 a.m.	212-627-9747 www.nycbestbar. com/downthehatch/	Beware of the low ceiling in this rowdy dive bar. Try to score a seat on the indoor swing. Go for wings and the amazing deals on everything! It's just plain fun.
Mon–Fri 4 p.m.–4 a.m. Sat–Sun 10:30 a.m.– 4 a.m.	646-638-2990 www.dublin6nyc. com	The $3 sliders, meatball sliders and kobe pigs in a blanket are tasty. Entrees include burgers and grilled fish. Brunch comes with two FREE drinks. It has a combination vibe of an Irish pub and a rustic farmhouse.
Mon–Wed 12 p.m.–12 a.m. Thu–Fri 12 p.m.–1 a.m. Sat–Sun 11:30 a.m.– 12 a.m.	212-260-2922 www.dukesnyc.com	The neon signs will lure you in but the food will keep you coming back! Good barbecue with plenty of seating and a fun atmosphere. Think large portions and Tex-Mex comfort food. Try the chili and the Kansas City ribs.

WHAT	DEAL	LOCATION
102 Duke's Barbecue Restaurant (2 locations)	4 p.m.–7 p.m. Monday–Friday ½ price drafts, bottles, specialty cocktails	560 Third Avenue (at 37th Street) Grand Central–42 St (4, 5, 6, 6X, 7, 7X) 33 St (4, 6, 6X) MURRAY HILL
Sports specials, trivia nights, beer pong		
103 Ear Inn Bar	4 p.m.–7 p.m. Monday–Friday $1 off bar	326 Spring Street (between Greenwich & Washington Streets) Houston St (1, 2) Canal St (1, 2) Spring St (A, C, E) SOHO
Live music, one of the oldest bars in New York City		
104 East Pacific Pan-Asian Bistro Asian Restaurant	11 a.m.–8 p.m. Monday–Friday ½ price drinks	120 East 34th Street (between Park & Lexington Avenues) 33 St (4, 6, 6X) 28 St (4, 6, 6X) Grand Central–42 St (7, 7X) EMPIRE STATE BUILDING
Food specials		

MONICA DiNATALE

HOURS	CONTACT	365 EXTRAS
Mon–Wed 12 p.m.–12 a.m. Thu–Fri 12 p.m.–1 a.m. Sat–Sun 11:30 a.m.– 12 a.m.	212-949-5400 www.dukesnyc.com	The neon signs will lure you in but the food will keep you coming back! Good barbecue with plenty of seating and a fun atmosphere. Think large portions and Tex-Mex comfort food. Try the chili and the Kansas City ribs.
Daily 12 p.m.–4 a.m.	212-431-9750 www.earinn.com	It was built in 1817 and is a designated landmark of New York City. Good burgers and reasonable menu all around. It definitely has rustic charm. Cozy, inviting and full of locals with backstories.
Mon–Thu 11:30 a.m.– 10:30 p.m. Fri–Sat 11:30 a.m.– 11:30 p.m. Sun 11:30 a.m.– 10 p.m.	212-696-2818	The curries and pad thai are flavorful and spicy. I appreciate the $4 appetizers. Try a mango martini and the boneless ribs. The sushi roll combos are a good deal as well.

	WHAT	DEAL	LOCATION
105	**East Village Tavern** Bar & Restaurant	12 p.m.–7 p.m. Monday–Friday $3 Bud & Bud Light bottles $4 well $4–$5 drafts $2 sliders $4 select drafts after 7 p.m.	158 Avenue C (at 10th Street) 1 Av (L) EAST VILLAGE
	Visiting breweries, pool table, open-mic nights		
106	**Ed's Chowder House** Seafood Restaurant	4 p.m.–6 p.m. Monday–Thursday $1 little neck clams $2 oysters $4 fried clams $3 Bud & Bud Light bottles $7 wine, Cosmos, martinis	4 West 63rd Street (between Broadway & Columbus Avenue) 59 St–Columbus Circle (1, 2, A, B, C, D) 66 St–Lincoln Center (1, 2) 72 St (A, B, C) LINCOLN CENTER
	Special occasion restaurant, across the street from Lincoln Center		
107	**El Azteca** Mexican Restaurant	4 p.m.–7 p.m. daily $4 beer $5 margaritas & sangria	783 Ninth Avenue (at 52nd Street) 50 St (A, C, E, 1, 2) 7 Av (B, D, E) HELL'S KITCHEN/ MIDTOWN WEST
	$12.95 brunch includes a FREE half pitcher of sangria, Bloody Mary or lime frozen margarita.		

MONICA DiNATALE

HOURS	CONTACT	365 EXTRAS
Mon–Fri 11:30 a.m.– 2 a.m. Sat–Sun 11 a.m.–2 a.m.	212-253-8400 www.evtnyc.com	Seventeen beers on tap and cask ale. Good bar food, burgers and chicken fingers. Unlimited booze brunch on weekends for one hour. You won't find specialty martinis just locals with a relaxed attitude.
Daily 11:30 a.m.– 10 p.m.	212-956-1288 www.chinagrillmgt. com	Excellent raw bar and tall bar tables that are first-come, first-served. The menu is upscale seafood. It is a beautiful spot for food or drinks before taking in a show at Lincoln Center.
Mon–Thu, Sun 11:30 a.m.– 12 a.m. Fri–Sat 11:30 a.m.– 1 a.m.	212-307-0616	FREE chips and salsa with drinks and dinner plus huge margaritas in many flavors. Drinks are always reasonable around $7. I like to sit in the window and order chicken mole.

	WHAT	DEAL	LOCATION
108	**El Cantinero** Mexican Restaurant	5 p.m.–12 a.m. Monday–Thursday, 5 p.m.–8 p.m. Saturday, Sunday all day $4 margaritas, beer, wine, sangria, house liquors	86 University Place (between 11th & 12th Streets) 14 St–Union Sq (4, 5, 6, 6X, L, N, Q, R) UNION SQUARE
	FREE appetizers Monday–Thursday (5 p.m.–7 p.m.), DJ		
109	**El Parador Café** Mexican Restaurant	3 p.m.–6 p.m. Monday–Saturday $5 beer, sangria & margaritas ½ price appetizers	325 East 34th Street (between 1st & 2nd Avenues) 33 St (4, 6, 6X) Grand Central–42 St (7, 7X) MURRAY HILL
	$20 three-course prix-fixe lunch Monday–Saturday 12p.m.–3p.m.		
110	**El Paso Restaurante** Mexican Restaurant (3 locations)	3 p.m.–7 p.m. Monday–Friday $1.25 tacos 4 p.m.–7 p.m. Monday–Friday $4 beer & sangria $5 margaritas	237 East 116th Street (between 2nd & 3rd Avenues) 116 St (4, 6, 6X) 125 St (4, 5, 6, 6X) HARLEM
	Tequila flights, food specials		

HOURS	CONTACT	365 EXTRAS
Mon–Wed, Sun 11:30 a.m.– 12 a.m. Thu 11:30 a.m.– 2 a.m. Fri–Sat 11:30 a.m.– 4 a.m.	212-255-9378 www.elcantineronyc. com	Go to the upstairs bar for the specials. You can make a meal of the FREE appetizers, and FREE chips and salsa come with drink orders. The music will make you want to dance.
Mon–Fri 11 a.m.–12 a.m. Sat–Sun 11 a.m.–1 a.m.	212-679-6812 www.elparadorcafe. com	Quite a find near the entrance to the Queens-Midtown Tunnel! Extensive tequila list and fun drink menu. Try the lamb tacos. Copper lighting and red accents make this a good date spot.
Daily 10:30 a.m.– 12 a.m.	212-860-4875 www.elpasony.com	It doesn't get any more authentic. Food is homemade and it shows. Definitely try the al pastor tacos and the mole sauce. Their micheladas and margaritas are another reason to return.

WHAT	DEAL	LOCATION
El Paso Restaurante Mexican Restaurant (3 locations)	3 p.m.–7 p.m. Monday–Friday $1 oysters $4 drafts $5 sangria $6 margaritas	1643 Lexington Avenue (between 103rd & 104th Streets) 103 St (4, 6, 6X) HARLEM/ UPPER EAST SIDE
Tequila flights, food specials		
El Paso Restaurante Mexican Restaurant (3 locations)	3 p.m.–6 p.m. Monday–Friday $4 beer $6 wine & margaritas	64 East 97th Street (between Park & Madison Avenues) 96 St (4, 6, 6X) HARLEM/ UPPER EAST SIDE
Emerald Pub Irish Pub	5 p.m.–8 p.m. Monday–Friday ½ price drinks	308 Spring Street (between Renwick & Greenwich Streets) Houston St (1, 2) Canal St (1, 2) Spring St (A, C, E) SOHO
They offer FREE grilled food throughout the summer like burgers and hot dogs. (Thursdays and Fridays)		

110

110

111

MONICA DiNATALE

HOURS	CONTACT	365 EXTRAS
Daily 11 a.m.–12 a.m.	212-831-9831 www.elpasony.com	It doesn't get any more authentic. Food is homemade and it shows. Definitely try the al pastor tacos and the mole sauce. Their micheladas and margaritas are another reason to return.
Daily 10:30 a.m.–12 a.m.	212-996-1739 www.elpasony.com	
Daily 11 a.m.–4 a.m.	212-226-8512 www.emerald-pubnyc.com	A very friendly Irish pub with a fireplace. You can reserve the back room with no fee for parties. The jukebox plays classic rock and the bartenders are always smiling. Check website for rotating specials and live music.

WHAT	DEAL	LOCATION
112 Empanada Mama H.K. Mexican Restaurant & Unique Empanadas	3 p.m.–6 p.m. & 1 a.m.–4 a.m. Monday–Thursday $5 frozen margaritas, sangria & beer	763 Ninth Avenue **(between 51st & 52nd Streets)** 50 St (A, C, E, 1, 2) 7 Av (B, D, E) HELL'S KITCHEN/ MIDTOWN WEST
Dozens of corn and wheat empanadas, good margaritas		
113 Empire Room Lounge	4 p.m.–7 p.m. daily $5 popcorn $6 beer $7 wine $8 cocktails & quesadillas	350 Fifth Avenue **(enter on 33rd Street, between Fifth & Madison Avenues)** 34 St–Herald Sq (B, D, F, M, N, Q, R) 33 St (4, 6, 6X) 28 St (N, R) EMPIRE STATE BUILDING
In the Empire State Building		
114 Emporio Italian Restaurant & Bar	5 p.m.– 6:30 p.m. daily $4.50 drafts & wine $6.50 cocktail specials FREE appetizers	231 Mott Street **(between Spring & Prince Streets)** Spring St (4, 6, 6X) Prince St (N, R) Bowery (J) SOHO
$16 weekend brunch includes one FREE Bloody Mary, mimosa or bellini.		

MONICA DiNATALE

HOURS	CONTACT	365 EXTRAS
Daily 10 a.m.–10 p.m.	212-698-9008 www.empmamanyc.com	Absolutely delicious empanadas. Try the Elvis with peanut butter and bananas and the cheese steak. At less than $3 a pop, you can sample many different flavors. This place is unique with outstanding food.
Daily 3 p.m. –1 a.m.	212-643-5400 www.facebook.com/theempireroom	Enjoy power cocktails with the rich and famous! This place is a find because of it's location, on the ground floor of the Empire State Building. Beautiful and classy with an upscale drink menu. Treat yourself.
Mon–Wed 12 p.m.–11 p.m. Thu–Fri 12 p.m.–12 a.m. Sat 11 a.m.–12 a.m. Sun 11 a.m.–10:30 p.m.	212-966-1234 www.emporiony.com	You must try one of their thin-crust pizzas. Broccoli rabe and sausage or the burrata are amazing. It is adorable and feels like an authentic Italian farmhouse. Perfect for a date. Homemade pastas.

WHAT	DEAL	LOCATION
115 **Entwine** Wine Bar & Restaurant	4 p.m.–7 p.m. Tuesday–Friday ½ price wine, sangria & well Monday ½ price bottles Sunday $8 wine	765 Washington Street (between Bethune & 12th Streets) 8 Av (L) Christopher St–Sheridan Sq (1, 2) 14 St (1, 2, 3) THE VILLAGE
Cocktail and bourbon menus		
116 **Epstein's Bar** Bar	4 p.m.–7 p.m. Thursday–Friday $3 beer, wine & well ½ price appetizers	82 Stanton Street (between Allen & Orchard Streets) 2 Av (F) Delancey St (F) Essex St (J, M, Z) LOWER EAST SIDE
Tuesday 2-for-1, lunch, dinner and drinks		
117 **Esperanto** Brazilian/South American Restaurant	4 p.m.–7 p.m. Monday–Friday Buy-1-get-1 FREE mojitos, caipirinha (per person) $3 chips and salsa	145 Avenue C (at 9th Street) 1 Av (L) EAST VILLAGE
$19.95 prix-fixe dinners Monday–Thursday until 7:30 p.m., Friday–Saturday until 6:30 p.m.		

MONICA DiNATALE

HOURS	CONTACT	365 EXTRAS
Daily 5:30 p.m. – 11 p.m.	212-727-8765 www.entwinenyc.com	I love this small but very inviting bar with cozy lounge seating in the back and an outdoor patio. They offer small plates perfect for sharing over wine. Try the stuffed dates with blue cheese.
Daily 11 a.m.–4 a.m.	212-477-2232 www.epsteins-barnyc.com	$13.50 brunch on weekends with all-you-can-drink specials on mimosas, screwdrivers and Bloody Marys until 2 p.m. are a good deal. It's an attractive neighborhood bar with good music and tons of drink specials.
Mon–Wed 5:30 p.m.– 12 a.m. Thu 12 p.m.– 12 a.m. Fri 12 p.m.– 2:30 a.m. Sat 11 a.m.– 1 a.m. Sun 11 a.m.– 12 a.m.	212-505-6559 www.esperantony.com	I like the empanadas and the carne asada. Try the fish tacos if you're in the mood for something lighter and, of course, a caipirinha. $11 brunch includes coffee and one drink.

| 118 | **Fetch**
Bar & Restaurant | 4:30 p.m.–
6:30 p.m.
Monday–Friday

½ price beer &
well | 1649 Third
Avenue
(between 92nd & 93rd
Streets)
96 St (4, 6, 6X)
86 St (4, 5, 6, 6X)

UPPER EAST
SIDE |

FREE dinner on your birthday

| 119 | **Fiddlesticks**
Irish Pub | 4 p.m.–8 p.m.
Monday–Friday

Sunday all day

$4 beer | 56 Greenwich
Avenue
(at Perry Street)
14 St (1, 2, 3)
Christopher St–Sheri-
dan Sq (1, 2)
8 Av (L)

THE VILLAGE |

Tons of sports specials

| 120 | **Finnerty's**
Pub & Restaurant | 4 p.m.–8 p.m.
Monday–Friday

$3 drafts &
bottles
$4 well | 221 Second
Avenue
(between 13th & 14th
Streets)
3Av (L)
1 Av (L)
14 St Union Sq (4, 5,
6, 6X)

EAST VILLAGE |

Fifteen beers on tap, special events

MONICA DiNATALE

HOURS	CONTACT	365 EXTRAS
Mon–Thu 11 a.m.–11 p.m. Fri 11 a.m.–12 a.m. Sat 10 a.m.–12 a.m. Sun 10 a.m.–11 p.m.	212-289-2700 www.fetchbarand-grill.com	Bring in a photo of your dog and it will go up on the wall, as the name would imply. They support no-kill shelters. Comfort food at its best.
Mon–Wed, Sun 11:30 a.m.–2 a.m. Thu–Sat 11:30 a.m.–4 a.m.	212-463-0516 www.fiddlesticksbar.com	It seems like it's been there forever! Great looking large rustic wood bar with brick walls and a pub menu. The Jameson fries are unique and tasty. They carry all sporting events and book parties at no charge.
Daily 12 p.m.–4 a.m.	212-677-2655 www.finnertysnyc.com	You can rent your own keg with a personal HD TV. Now that's a party! This is a San Francisco teams bar with many different sports specials. Bring your own food and spend the day with your friends from the west coast.

	WHAT	DEAL	LOCATION
121	**Fish Restaurant** Seafood Restaurant	Daily $8 for 6 oysters or clams & a glass of wine or PBR	280 Bleecker Street **(between Jones and Commerce Streets)** **Christopher St–Sheridan Sq (1, 2)** **W 4 St (A, B, C, D, E, F, M)** **Houston St (1, 2)** THE VILLAGE
	FREE peanuts at the bar, dinner and lunch specials		
122	**Five Points** Bar & Restaurant	5:30 p.m.– 7:30 p.m. daily $5 drinks $6 snacks	31 Great Jones Street **(between Lafayette & Bowery Streets)** **Bleecker St (4, 6, 6X)** **Broadway–Lafayette St (B, D, F, M)** **8 St–Nyu (N, R)** NOHO
	Unique cocktail menu, $24 three-course lunch		
123	**Flex Mussels** Seafood Restaurant **(2 locations)**	5:30 p.m.– 7 p.m. daily at bar & counter $25 for 2 pots of mussels (3 types), 2 pots of fries & 1 beer or wine	154 West 13th Street **(between 6th & 7th Avenues)** **14 St (1, 2, 3, F, M)** **6 Av (L)** UNION SQUARE
	Twenty plus sauces for mussels		

MONICA DiNATALE

HOURS	CONTACT	365 EXTRAS
Sun–Thu 12 p.m.–11 p.m. Fri–Sat 12 p.m.–12 a.m.	212-727-2879 www.fishrestaurantnyc.com	The delicious fresh seafood keeps them packed. It's worth the wait if there are crowds! I often go for just oysters, clams and shrimp. I like the bar area if you can score a seat.
Mon–Fri 12 p.m.–11 p.m. Sat–Sun 11 a.m.– 11:30 p.m.	212-253-5700 www.fivepoints-restaurant.com	Wonderful upscale local fresh menu in a beautiful dining room with an open kitchen. They make me feel like I'm in Paris. The lemon ricotta pancakes and the potato pizza with truffle oil are excellent.
Mon–Thu 5 p.m.–11 p.m. Fri–Sat 5 p.m.–12 a.m. Sun 5 p.m.–10 p.m.	212-229-0222 www.flexmusselsny.com	To-die-for mussels. Even if you think you don't like them, go! I've converted many people. Get there early for the specials. The 82nd Street location has the most bar seating. Splurge for the Thai curry or the fra diavolo flavors.

123	**Flex Mussels** Seafood Restaurant **(2 locations)**	5:30 p.m.– 7 p.m. daily at bar & counter $25 for 2 pots of mussels **(3 types)**, 2 pots of fries and 1 beer or wine	174 East 82nd Street **(between 3rd & Lexington Avenues)** 77 St & 86 St (6) UPPER EAST SIDE
	Twenty plus sauces for mussels		
124	**Flight 151** Bar	5 p.m.–7 p.m. Monday–Friday $1.50 domestic mugs $3 well	151 Eighth Avenue **(between 17th & 18th Streets)** 14 St (A, C, E) 8 Av (L) 18 St (1, 2) CHELSEA
	Jukebox		
125	**Foley's** Irish Pub	Daily $5 drafts & Cosmos $6 well $18–$25 beer buckets **(5)**	18 West 33rd Street **(between 5th Avenue & Broadway)** 34 St–Herald Sq (B, D, F, M, N, Q, R) 28 St (N, R) 33 St (4, 6, 6X) MADISON SQUARE GARDEN/PENN STATION
	Irish breakfast all day, sports specials		

90

HOURS	CONTACT	365 EXTRAS
Mon–Thu 5:30 p.m.– 11:00 p.m. Fri 5:30 p.m.– 11:30 p.m. Sat 5 p.m.– 11:30 p.m. Sun 5 p.m.– 10 p.m.	212-717-7772 www.flexmusselsny. com	To-die-for mussels. Even if you think you don't like them, go! I've converted many people. Get there early for the specials. The 82nd Street location has the most bar seating. Splurge for the Thai curry or the fra diavolo flavors.
Sun–Thu 11 a.m.–1 a.m. Fri–Sat 11 a.m.–2 a.m.	212-229-1868	Casual airplane-themed place. Very comfortable with solid bar food, good curly fries, and a chilled vibe. If you want to relax the day away, give this place a try. No attitudes.
Mon–Wed 10 a.m.–2 a.m. Thu 10 a.m.–3 a.m. Fri–Sat 10 a.m.–4 a.m. Sun 11 a.m.–1 a.m.	212-290-0080 www.foleysny.com	So much baseball memorabilia that you'll feel like you're in Cooperstown. The walls, menu, name of dishes–everything– makes this a baseball lover's dream and great family place to visit. A must for sports fans.

WHAT	DEAL	LOCATION
126 **Fontana's Bar** Bar	2 p.m.–8 p.m. daily $3 drafts $4 vodka & gin drinks $5 wine & Bloody Marys $6 lager & shot	105 Eldridge Street (between Broome & Grand Streets) Grand St (B, D) Bowery (J) Delancey St (F) LOWER EAST SIDE
FREE live music seven days a week, jukebox		
127 **Fresh Salt** Restaurant & Bar	4 p.m.–8 p.m. daily $4 drafts & well	146 Beekman Street (between Front & South Streets) Wall St (2, 3) Fulton St (A, C, J, Z, 2, 3) SOUTH STREET SEAPORT
Weekend brunch, delicious homemade meatloaf		
128 **Fulton** Seafood Restaurant & Bar	5 p.m.–7 p.m. daily $.50 clams $1 oysters $4 beer $6 wine, gin & vodka drinks	205 East 75th Street (at 3rd Avenue) 77 St (4, 6, 6X) 68 St–Hunter College (4, 6, 6X) UPPER EAST SIDE
Dinner specials, good raw bar, outdoor heated seating		

MONICA DiNATALE

HOURS	CONTACT	365 EXTRAS
Daily 2 p.m.–4 a.m.	212-334-6740 www.fontanasnyc. com	It is a find located among a sea of Chinese restaurants. No cover music every day. There are three levels with a pool table in the basement. Take a picture in the photo booth to show your friends.
Daily 10 a.m.–4 a.m.	212-962-0053 www.freshsalt.com	Blink and you may miss this hidden gem tucked away on Beekman Street. The rustic dining room matches a casual pita sandwich and salads menu. The prices are always reasonable and the staff friendly.
Mon–Sat 11:30 a.m.– 10 p.m. Sun 10:30 a.m.– 9 p.m.	212-288-6600 www.fultonnyc.com	The truffle parm popcorn is addictive. Nice raw bar and upscale seafood menu. I go for the $1 oysters but the pink snapper is delicious. Lounge atmosphere with cool jazz playing all night long.

	WHAT	DEAL	LOCATION
129	**Gaf West** Bar	5 p.m.–7 p.m. daily $3 drafts $4 well	401 West 48th Street (between 9th & 10th Avenues) 50 St (A, C, E, 1, 2) 42 St–Port Authority Bus Terminal (A, C, E) HELL'S KITCHEN/ MIDTOWN WEST
	Darts, jukebox		
130	**Galway Hooker** Bar & Restaurant	4 p.m.–8 p.m. Monday–Friday $4 drafts, bottles, wine & well	133 Seventh Avenue South (between Charles & 10th Streets) Christopher St–Sheridan Sq (1, 2) W 4 St (A, B, C, D, E, F, M) 14 St (1, 2, 3) THE VILLAGE
	Fireplace, sports specials		
131	**Garden Café** Bar & Restaurant	11 a.m.–6 p.m. Monday–Friday $3 beer $4 mimosas $5 wine & sangria	4961 Broadway (at 207th Street) Inwood–207 St (A) 207 St (1) 215 St (1) INWOOD
	Outdoor seating, food specials		

HOURS	CONTACT	365 EXTRAS
Daily 5 p.m.–4 a.m.	212-307-7536 www.gafwestnyc.com	The perfect "gaf" or bar to call home. It's comfortable like your own personal bar and filled with friendly locals. They don't serve food, but you can order in from nearby restaurants.
Mon–Wed, Sun 11:30 a.m.– 2 a.m. Thu–Sat 11:30 a.m.– 4 a.m.	212-675-6220 www.galwayhooker-bar.com	Three words– oatmeal cookie martini! I think it's a combination of a lounge with an Irish Pub feel plus a creative drink menu. I like to relax on the couches upstairs. Try the Jameson fries and a burger.
Mon–Fri 11 a.m.–11 p.m. Sat–Sun 10 a.m.–11 p.m.	212-544-9480	Gorgeous outdoor café with a comfortable bar and small tables. Think French bistro in New York City. They have a moderately priced menu, reasonable drinks, and good sandwiches. Relax and enjoy.

	WHAT	DEAL	LOCATION
132	**Gatsby's** Bar & Restaurant	5 p.m.–7 p.m. Monday–Friday $4 drafts $6 wine $7 mojitos	53 Spring Street **(between Lafayette & Mulberry Streets) Spring St (4, 6, 6X) Prince St (N, R) Bowery (J)** SOHO
	Lounge seating, dinner specials		
133	**George Keeley Fine Ales & Lagers** Irish Pub	2 p.m.–8 p.m. Monday–Friday $1–$2 off bar	485 Amsterdam Avenue **(between 83rd & 84th Streets) 86 St (1, 2) 79 St (1, 2) 81 St–Museum of Natural History (A, B, C)** UPPER WEST SIDE
	Visiting breweries, sports specials		
134	**Georgia's Eastside BBQ** Barbecue Restaurant	3 p.m.–5 p.m. Monday–Friday $2 beer $5 sandwiches	192 Orchard Street **(between Houston & Stanton Streets) Delancey St & 2nd Ave (F) Essex St (J, M, Z)** LOWER EAST SIDE
	Creative hot dog menu		

HOURS	CONTACT	365 EXTRAS
Daily 11 a.m.–4 a.m.	212-334-4430 www.gatsbysnyc.com	Good beer selection and bar menu with tasty sliders, wings and chicken fingers, right in the heart of the Soho area. Definitely a reasonably priced sports bar in this neighborhood with a cozy atmosphere.
Mon–Fri 2 p.m.–4 a.m. Sat–Sun 12 p.m.–4 a.m.	212-873-0251 www.georgekeeley.com	Twenty plus beers on tap and FREE popcorn to keep you full. Register for the beer club to keep things interesting and maybe you'll get a plaque on the wall. I love the burgers with sweet potato fries, and the friendly bartenders.
Sun–Mon 10 a.m.–10 p.m. Tue–Sat 10 a.m.–11 p.m.	212-253-6280 www.georgiaseastsidebbq.com	Heavy Metal Home Cooking! The slogan says it all. The meat falls off the bone of the ribs and the sauces are amazing. There are only five tables and a small bar. Worth the wait.

WHAT	DEAL	LOCATION
135 **Great Jones Café** Cajun Restaurant & Bar	5 p.m.–7 p.m. Monday–Friday $3 drafts $1 off all other drinks	54 Great Jones Street (between Bowery & Lafayette Streets) Bleecker St (4, 6, 6X) Broadway–Lafayette St (B, D, F, M) Astor Pl (4, 6, 6X) NOHO
Menu changes daily, weekend brunch		
136 **Greenwich Street Tavern** Bar & Restaurant	5 p.m.–8 p.m. Monday–Friday ½ price beer, wine & well	399 Greenwich Street (between Beach & Hubert Streets) Franklin St (1, 2) Canal St (A, C, E, 1, 2) TRIBECA
Sports specials, outdoor seating		
137 **Greenwich Treehouse** Bar	5 p.m.–8 p.m. daily $1 off bottles $2 off drafts $4 well $5 margaritas $6 shot & beer	46 Greenwich Avenue (between Charles & Perry Streets) 14 St (1, 2, 3) Christopher St–Sheridan Sq (1, 2) 6 Av (L) THE VILLAGE
Stand-up comedy Wednesdays		

MONICA DiNATALE

HOURS	CONTACT	365 EXTRAS
Mon 5 p.m.–12 a.m. Tue–Thu 12 p.m.–12 a.m. Fri 12 p.m.–1 a.m. Sat 11:30 a.m.– 1 a.m. Sun 11:30 a.m.– 12 a.m.	212-674-9304 www.greatjones. com	Take a trip south without leaving New York City! The menu has a Cajun twist, delicious comfort food and everything is homemade. I like to order a few things and share. Try the jambalaya.
Mon 11 a.m.–10 p.m. Tue–Fri 11 a.m.–11 p.m. Sat 4 p.m.–11 p.m.	212-334-7827 www.greenwich- streettavernnyc.com	The casual menu includes boneless buffalo bites and salads. Think upscale sports bar with good sandwiches and wraps. It attracts the "financial" crowd after work so you might even pick up a good stock tip.
Mon–Wed 5 p.m.–12 a.m. Thu 5 p.m.–1 a.m. Fri–Sat 5 p.m.–4 a.m. Sun 3 p.m.–10 p.m.	212-675-0395 www.greenwichtree- house.com	It really is "a bar above it all." The Treehouse is perched on the second floor slightly hidden from the masses. It's a great dive bar with cheap drinks. I like to sit in the windows and watch the busy streets.

	WHAT	DEAL	LOCATION
138	**Guadalupe** Mexican Bar & Grill	3 p.m.–7 p.m. Monday–Friday Wednesday all day 2-for-1 drinks	597 West 207th Street **(between Broadway & Vermilyea Avenue)** **Inwood–207 St (A)** **207 St (1)** **215 St (1)** INWOOD
	Kids dinner menu $7, live music		
139	**Guayoyo** Venezuelan Restaurant & Bar	12 p.m.–8 p.m. Monday–Friday $4 beer $5 well $5 sangria FREE tapas	67 First Avenue **(at 4th Street)** **2 Av (F)** **Astor Pl (4, 6, 6X)** **Bleecker St (4, 6, 6X)** EAST VILLAGE
	Weekend brunch includes one FREE drink.		
140	**Gusto** Italian Restaurant	4 p.m.–7 p.m. daily $5 beers $7 cocktails & wine	60 Greenwich Avenue **(at 11th Street & 7th Avenue)** **14 St (1, 2, 3)** **Christopher St–Sheridan Sq (1, 2)** **6 Av (L)** THE VILLAGE
100	Monday $1 oysters, Tuesday 50% off wine bottles		

HOURS	CONTACT	365 EXTRAS
Sun–Thu 3 p.m.–12 a.m. Fri–Sat 3:30 p.m.–1 a.m.	212-304-1083 www.guadalupeba-randgrill.com	FREE live music Fridays and Sundays. Beware of the Guadalupe margaritas, they go down smooth and quick. Upscale Mexican menu with bright orange décor. Near the last stop on the A train.
Mon 4:30 p.m.–12 a.m. Tue–Thu 12 p.m.–12 a.m. Fri 12 p.m.–1 a.m. Sat 11 a.m.–1 a.m. Sun 11 a.m.–12 a.m.	212-979-6646 www.guayoyonyc.com	I can't get enough sweet plantains. The menu is reasonable and everything is homemade. Don't leave without sampling one of the "arepas" stuffed breads. They can be a meal.
Mon–Fri 11 a.m.–11 p.m. Sat–Sun 10 a.m.–11 p.m.	212-924-8000 www.gustonyc.com	Authentic Italian food in a beautiful upscale setting. I recommend the homemade pastas and the fried artichokes if you're staying for dinner. $22 brunch on weekends includes two courses and one hour of unlimited drinks.

WHAT	DEAL	LOCATION
Gyu-Kaku Japanese Barbecue & Bar (3 locations)	11:30 a.m.– 6 p.m. daily, 9:30 p.m.– 11 p.m. Monday– Thursday ½ price drinks & menu	34 Cooper Square (at 4th Avenue & 6th Street) Astor Pl (4, 6, 6X) 8 St-Nyu (N, R) Bleecker St (4, 6, 6X) EAST VILLAGE

Try grilling bananas for dessert!

WHAT	DEAL	LOCATION
Gyu-Kaku Japanese Barbecue & Bar (3 locations)	11:30 a.m.– 6 p.m. daily, 9:30 p.m.– 11 p.m. Monday– Thursday ½ price drinks & menu	805 Third Avenue, Second Floor (between 49th & 50th Streets) 51 St (4, 6, 6X) Lexington Av/53 St (E, M) Grand Central–42 St (7, 7X) MIDTOWN EAST

WHAT	DEAL	LOCATION
Gyu-Kaku Japanese Barbecue & Bar (3 locations)	11:30 a.m.– 6 p.m. daily, 9:30 p.m.– 11 p.m. Monday– Thursday ½ price drinks & menu	321 West 44th Street (between 8th & 9th Avenues) 42 St (1, 2, 3) TIMES SQUARE/ THEATER DISTRICT

HOURS	CONTACT	365 EXTRAS
Mon–Thu 11:30 a.m.– 11 p.m. Fri–Sat 11:30 a.m.– 12 a.m. Sun 11:30 a.m.– 10 p.m.	212-475-2989 www.gyu-kaku.com	Grilling your own meal is unique and satisfying. You can't beat half-price food specials. The restaurants are spacious and modern with a twist of bamboo. The steamers are built right into the tables.
Mon–Thu 11:30 a.m.– 10:30 p.m. Fri 11:30 a.m.– 11:30 p.m. Sat 12 p.m.– 11:30 p.m. Sun 12 p.m.– 9:30 p.m.	212-702-8816 www.gyu-kaku.com	
Mon–Thu 11:30 a.m.– 11 p.m. Fri–Sat 11:30 a.m.– 12 a.m. Sun 11:30 a.m.– 10 p.m.	646-692-9115 www.gyu-kaku.com	

WHAT	DEAL	LOCATION
142 **Hallo Berlin** German Restaurant & Beer Garden	4 p.m.–7 p.m. Monday–Friday $1 off beers & appetizers	626 Tenth Avenue (between 44th & 45th Streets) 42 St–Port Authority Bus Terminal (A, C, E) 50 St (A, C, E) HELL'S KITCHEN/ MIDTOWN WEST
Beer garden open year-round		
143 **Harlem Bar-B-Q** Barbecue Restaurant & Bar	4 p.m.–7 p.m. Monday– Thursday $3 drafts $4 well	2367 Frederick Douglas Boulevard (between 127th & 128th Streets) 125 St (A, B, C, D, 2, 3) 135 St (A, B, C) HARLEM
Frozen drink menu, private party room		
144 **Harry's Burritos** Mexican Restaurant	4 p.m.–7 p.m. daily $3.50 well, beer, margaritas	241 Columbus Avenue (at 71st Street) 72 St (A, B, C, 1, 2, 3) 66 St–Lincoln Center (1, 2) UPPER WEST SIDE
Outdoor seating, tequila menu		

MONICA DiNATALE

HOURS	CONTACT	365 EXTRAS
Mon–Sat 11 a.m.–11 p.m. Sun 4 p.m.–11 p.m.	212-977-1944 www.halloberlin-restaurant.com	They are the real deal! Lots of wurst, potato pancakes and, of course, a jumbo German pretzel. The waitresses are knowledgable about the twenty plus German beers.
Mon–Thu 12 p.m.–10 p.m. Fri–Sun 12 p.m.–11 p.m.	212-222-1922 www.harlembarbq.com	Great BBQ, combo platters, ribs, tradiional BBQ sides, and interesting flavors. Make the trip and be sure to arrive hungry! Afterwards check out all the shopping on 125th Street.
Sun–Thu 11 a.m.–12 a.m. Fri–Sat 11.30 a.m.– 1 a.m.	212-580-9494 www.harrysburritos.com	Large quesadillas stuffed with fresh ingredients. I go for the chicken wrapped in a spinach tortilla, and I love the jalapeño poppers. Drinks come in a variety of sizes and are potent so beware!

	WHAT	DEAL	LOCATION
145	**Havana Central** Cuban Restaurant & Bar (2 locations)	4 p.m.–7 p.m. Monday–Friday $1 empanadas $4 beer $5 wine $6 mojitos & margaritas $7 sangria	151 West 46th Street (between 6th & 7th Avenues) 49 St (N, Q, R) 47–50 Sts–Rockefeller Ctr (B, D, F, M) Times Sq–42 St (S) TIMES SQUARE/ THEATER DISTRICT/ MIDTOWN
	Sunday Salsa nights, live Latin music		
145	**Havana Central** Cuban Restaurant & Bar (2 locations)	3 p.m.–7 p.m. Monday–Friday $1 empanadas $3 beer $5 wine $6 mojitos & margaritas $7 sangria	2911 Broadway (between 113th & 114th Streets) 116 St–Columbia University (1) Cathedral Pkwy (1) MORNINGSIDE HEIGHTS
146	**Hearth** Wine Bar	5:30 p.m.– 6:30 p.m. daily $4 bar snacks $7 wine	413 East 12th Street (between 1st Avenue & Avenue A) 1 Av (L) 3 Av (L) Astor Pl (4, 6, 6X) EAST VILLAGE
	Wine list from around the world		

MONICA DiNATALE

HOURS	CONTACT	365 EXTRAS
Mon–Wed, Sun 11:30 a.m.– 11 p.m. Thu–Sat 11:30 a.m.– 12 a.m.	212-398-7440 www.havanacentral. com	The empanadas and Cuban sandwiches are fresh and flavorful. Fun and lively, they book Latin bands for entertainment. Check website for schedules. Make a reservation, you'll want to keep eating!
Mon–Wed, Sun 11:30 a.m.– 10 p.m. Thu 11:30 a.m.– 11 p.m. Fri–Sat 11:30 a.m.– 12 a.m.	212-662-8830 www.havanacentral. com	
Mon–Sat 5 p.m.–2 a.m. Sun 5 p.m.–12 a.m.	212-625-WINE (9463) www.wineisterroir. com	This was the location of the orginal Terrior Wine Bar and a blueprint for knowledgable staff and friendly service. They make picking a wine fun. Comfortable and classy.

	WHAT	DEAL	LOCATION
147	**Hi-Fi** Bar	Until 8 p.m. daily $3 beer & well $4 wine $2 off bar until 12 a.m. daily $4 drink specials	169 Avenue A **(between 10th & 11th Streets)** 1 Av (L) 2 Av (F) Astor Pl (4, 6, 6X) EAST VILLAGE
	Jukebox, DJ, pool table		
148	**Holland Bar** Bar	Daily $2 beers	532 Ninth Avenue **(between 39th & 40th Streets)** 42 St–Times Sq (A, C, E, 7, 7X) 34 St–Penn Station (A, C, E) HELL'S KITCHEN/ MIDTOWN WEST TIMES SQUARE/ THEATER DISTRICT
	Sports specials, jukebox		
149	**Hundred Acres** Bar & Restaurant	5:30 p.m.– 7 p.m. Monday–Friday $3 beer $6 cocktails & appetizers	38 MacDougal Street **(between Houston & Prince Streets)** Spring St (A, C, E) Houston St (1, 2) Prince St (N, R) SOHO
108	Private parties and a chef's table		

HOURS	CONTACT	365 EXTRAS
Mon–Thu 4 p.m.–4 a.m. Fri–Sat 3 p.m.–4 a.m.	212-420-8392 www.thehifibar.com	It's a fun space in the East Village with an indie rock jukebox. Prices are always reasonable with an even better extended happy hour. Small but comfortable with no frills.
Daily 8 a.m.–4 a.m.	212-502-4609	Always flush with New York regulars day and night because of it's location near Times Square. Cheap drinks, amazing conversations and fast service. A good place to take a load off and grab a beer.
Mon–Fri 12 p.m.–12 a.m. Sat 11 a.m.–12 a.m. Sun 11 a.m.–10 p.m.	212-475-7500 www.hundredacres-nyc.com	It feels like a French farmhouse with home cooking. The upscale American menu has a Cajun twist. They offer ten plus whiskeys and whiskey flights. Try the chipotle margarita for something different.

WHAT	DEAL	LOCATION
I Tre Merli Italian Restaurant & Bar	4 p.m.–8 p.m. Monday–Friday FREE appetizers at the bar	463 West Broadway (between Houston & Prince Streets) Spring St (A, C, E) Prince St (N, R) Broadway–Lafayette St (B, D, F, M) SOHO
Private party room, homemade favorites		
Iggy's Bar & Restaurant	5 p.m.–7 p.m. Monday–Friday $3 domestic bottles & pints $5 well	1452 Second Avenue (between 75th & 76th Streets) 77 St (4, 6, 6X) 68 St–Hunter College (4, 6, 6X) UPPER EAST SIDE
Karaoke, live music, children's karaoke parties		
ilili Mediterranean Restaurant	5:30 p.m.–7:30 p.m. Monday–Friday ½ price drinks & appetizers	236 Fifth Avenue (between 27th & 28th Streets) 28 St (4, 6, 6X, N, R) 23 St (N, R) FLATIRON/GRAMERCY
Prix-fixe menus, dinner specials		

150
151
152

MONICA DiNATALE

HOURS	CONTACT	365 EXTRAS
Sun–Wed 12 p.m.–11 p.m. Thu–Sat 12 p.m.–12 a.m.	212-254-8699 www.itremerli.com	Brick walls, skylights and red accents make this a nice romantic place. Homemade pastas and an extensive wine list will keep you coming back for more. Try the gnocchi with pesto. Impress your date.
Daily 11:30 a.m.– 4 a.m.	212-327-3043 www.iggysnewyork.com	Small with a no frills dive bar attitude. Karaoke is the star here. It's a fun place to hang out with plenty of entertainment from karaoke pros. Give it a try if you dare!
Sun–Wed 12 p.m.– 10:30 p.m. Thu–Sat 12 p.m.– 11:30 p.m.	212-683-2929 www.ililinyc.com	Super modern room with slate floors and cool jazz playing. Authentic falafel, hummus and kafta lead the Mediterranean menu. It's the kind of food that is perfect for sharing. Everything here is flavorful and fresh.

WHAT	DEAL	LOCATION
153 **Il Punto** Italian Restaurant	5 p.m.–7 p.m. Monday–Friday, 12 p.m.–8 p.m. Saturday, Sunday all day $4 beer $5 wine $6.50 sangria Tuesdays all night $6 martinis	**507 Ninth Avenue** (at 38th Street) 42 St–Port Authority Bus Terminal (A, C, E) 34 St–Penn Station (A, C, E) Times Sq–42 St (7, 7X) **HELL'S KITCHEN/ MIDTOWN WEST**
Homemade pastas		
154 **Indian Road Café** Restaurant & Coffee Bar	4 p.m.–6 p.m. daily 2-for-1 beer & wine	**600 West 218th Street** (at Indian Road) 215 St (1) Inwood–207 St (A) Marble Hill–225 St (1) **INWOOD**
Live music, open-mic nights		
155 **International Bar** Bar	Daily $2 beer $4 well	**120 ½ First Avenue** (between 7th & 8th Streets) 1 Av (L) 2 Av (F) Astor Pl (4, 6, 6X) **EAST VILLAGE**
Backyard patio, jukebox		

MONICA DiNATALE

HOURS	CONTACT	365 EXTRAS
Mon–Thu, Sun 11:30 a.m.–11 p.m. Fri–Sat 11:30 a.m.–12 a.m.	212-244-0088 www.ilpuntonyc.com	White tablecloth Italian dining with homemade pastas and FREE mini biscotti after dinner. Service is excellent. The branzino is a good choice if you want to splurge.
Mon–Thu 7 a.m.–10 p.m. Fri–Sat 7 a.m.–11 p.m. Sun 8 a.m.–10 p.m.	212-942-7451 www.indianroadcafe.com	Location, location, location. They are perfectly positioned next to Inwood Hill Park and Columbia University's sports complex. Eat in or plan your picnic. This place is a unique combination of bar and coffee bar.
Daily 8 a.m.–4 a.m.	212-777-1643 www.internationalbarnyc.com	Small, cheap, dark and friendly. Enough said. A perfect hole in the wall for an affordable long night of drinking and conversation. Leave your tie at home.

156	**Iron Horse NYC** Bar & Restaurant	Daily $2 PBR & Rolling Rock 11:30 a.m.–8 p.m. daily $4 domestic bottles $5 import bottles & vodka $6 shot & beer combos	**32 Cliff Street** (between Fulton & John Streets) Fulton St (A, C, J, Z, 2, 3) Wall St (2, 3) **FINANCIAL DISTRICT**
	Rotating specials like FREE hot dogs and $10 burger and pint		
157	**Jack Demsey's** Bar & Restaurant	5 p.m.–8 p.m. daily $4 drafts $7 well	**36 West 33rd Street** (between Broadway & 5th Avenue) 34 St–Herald Sq (1, 2, 3, B, D, F, M, N, Q, R) **MADISON SQUARE GARDEN/ PENN STATION**
	Soccer, sports specials, live music		
158	**Jack Russell's Pub** Bar & Restaurant	Until 7 p.m. daily $3 pints $4 Jägermeister shots $10 pitchers	**1591 Second Avenue** (between 82nd & 83rd Streets) 86 St (4, 5, 6, 6X) 77 St (4, 6, 6X) **UPPER EAST SIDE**
	Thirteen HD TVs, sports specials, pool tables, karaoke, ping-pong		

MONICA DiNATALE

HOURS	CONTACT	365 EXTRAS
Mon–Sat 11:30 a.m.– 4 a.m. Sun 12 p.m.–4 a.m.	646-546-5426 www.ironhorsenyc. com	A fun dive bar complete with dancing bartenders to keep things interesting. Reasonable burgers, bar food, and shots. They usually have classic rock playing or FREE live music. Very casual.
Daily 10 a.m.–4 a.m.	212-629-9899 www.jackdemseys. com	I love Irish pubs with Irish bartenders. With three floors, it's perfect for any size group. Good place to watch any of the games, including rugby and soccer. Irish breakfast every day and Guinness on tap.
Mon–Fri 4 p.m.–4 a.m. Sat–Sun 12 p.m.–4 a.m.	212-472-2800 www.jackrussell-snyc.com	They always offer good deals. You can see the games from every angle and if you're bored, try beer pong. Very spacious and comfortable. Sports lovers rejoice!

WHAT	DEAL	LOCATION
159 **Jake's Dilemma** Bar	4 p.m.–8 p.m. Monday– Thursday, 3 p.m.–8 p.m. Friday, 12 p.m.–8 p.m. Saturday– Sunday ½ price bar	430 Amsterdam Avenue (between 80th & 81st Streets) 79 St & 86 St (1, 2) 81 St–Museum of Natural History (A, B, C) UPPER WEST SIDE
Daily drink specials, outdoor seating, darts		
160 **Jake's Saloon** Pub & Restaurant	11 a.m.–7 p.m. Monday–Friday $3 Bud Light drafts, Miller Light $4 Jake's Tricky Ale $5–$6 Cosmos, well $6 wine	206 West 23rd Street (at 7th Avenue) 23 St (A, C, E, 1, 2) 14 St (A, C, E) CHELSEA
Sports specials, dinner specials		
161 **Jameson's** Irish Pub	3 p.m.–8 p.m. daily $4 domestic beers $5 imported beers & well	975 Second Avenue (between 51st & 52nd Streets) Lexington Av/53 St (E, M) 51 St (4, 6, 6X) 59 St (4, 5, 6, 6X) MIDTOWN EAST
Fox® Sports Soccer Channel		

116

HOURS	CONTACT	365 EXTRAS
Mon–Thu 4 p.m.–4 a.m. Fri 3 p.m.–4 a.m. Sat–Sun 12 p.m.–4 a.m.	212-580-0556 www.nycbestbar.com/jakes/	It's hard to keep track of all the rotating specials. You will definitely find something you like and save money. Try the mac n' cheese but most people go for the burger.
Mon–Wed 5 p.m.–2 a.m. Thu–Sun 11 a.m.–4 a.m.	212-337-3100 www.jakessaloonnyc.com	Modern and spacious, they serve large portions of sandwiches and salads. Good bar crowd after work. Although there are two other locations, the deals here make this spot stand out!
Mon–Fri 12 p.m.–12 a.m. Sat–Sun 12 p.m.–4 a.m.	212-980-4465 www.jamesonsny.com	Great old-world pub atmosphere right out of Ireland. The menu is always reasonable and includes Irish favorites and sports specials. You will want to chill at a table all night. Weekend brunch includes one FREE beverage.

	WHAT	DEAL	LOCATION
162	**Jeremy's Ale House** Bar & Restaurant	4 p.m.–6 p.m. Monday–Friday $1.50 Coors pints $5 32 oz. beer ½ price well	**228 Front Street** (between Beekman Street & Peck Slip) Fulton St (A, C, J, Z, 2, 3) Wall St (2, 3) SOUTH STREET SEAPORT
	Outdoor seating, jukebox		
163	**Jimmy's Corner** Bar	Daily $3 beers	**140 West 44th Street** (between Broadway & 7th Avenue) Times Sq–42 St (1, 2, 3, N, Q, R, S) 42 St–Bryant Pk (B, D, F, M) TIMES SQUARE/ THEATER DISTRICT
	Close to Times Square, jukebox		
164	**Johnny Utah's** Southwestern Restaurant	4 p.m.–10 p.m. daily $2 Rolling Rock, Busch Beer $3 Coors, Bud drafts $5 margaritas, frozen & on the rocks	**25 West 51st Street** (between 5th & 6th Avenues) 47–50 Sts–Rockefeller Ctr (B, D, F, M) 5 Av/53 St (E, M) 7 Av (B, D, E) RADIO CITY/ ROCKEFELLER CENTER
	Mechanical bull riding, revolving dinner specials		

118

HOURS	CONTACT	365 EXTRAS
Mon–Thu 8 a.m.–12 a.m. Fri 8 a.m.–1 a.m. Sat 10 a.m.–1 a.m. Sun 12 p.m.–12 a.m.	212-964-3537 www.jeremysale-house.com	Appetizers start at $3 and sandwiches at $4. It's a styrofoam cup kind of place. Good fried food and bras hanging from the ceiling make for an interesting, good time crowd at happy hour and beyond.
Daily 11 a.m.–4 a.m.	212-221-9510	One of the remaining, classic dive bars in Times Square. No frills with lots of New York attitude and reasonable drink prices. A shrine to boxing with tons of photos lining the walls. It is across the street from the Hudson Theater.
Mon, Thu 11:30 a.m.–2 a.m. Tue–Wed 11:30 a.m.–1 a.m. Fri 11:30 a.m.–3 a.m. Sat 5 p.m.–3 a.m.	212-265-8824 www.johnnyutahs.com	Bull riding with the after work and evening crowd is something different and makes for great people watching. This place is huge and great for groups with table taps available for large parties.

	WHAT	DEAL	LOCATION
165	**Johnny's Bar** Bar	3 p.m.–7 p.m. daily Buy-2-get-1 FREE drinks $4.25 cocktails & well	90 Greenwich Avenue (at 12th Street) 8 Av (L) 14 St (A, C, E, 1, 2, 3) THE VILLAGE
	Interesting shot menu, drink specials		
166	**Karma** Hookah Bar	1 p.m.–9 p.m. Monday–Friday ½ price beer, wine & well	51 First Avenue (between 3rd & 4th Streets) 2 Av (F) Bleecker St (4, 6, 6X) Astor Pl (4, 6, 6X) EAST VILLAGE
	Cigarette smoking permitted, hookah menu		
167	**Keats** Bar & Restaurant	4 p.m.–7 p.m. Monday–Friday $3 Bud drafts & domestic bottles $6 appletini & Cosmos	842 Second Avenue (at 45th Street) Grand Central–42 St (4, 5, 6, 6X, 7, 7X) 51 St (4, 6, 6X) MIDTOWN EAST
120	Karaoke, private parties		

HOURS	CONTACT	365 EXTRAS
Daily 12 p.m.–4 a.m.	212-741-5279 www.johnnysbarnyc.com	Shots of the day are interesting! I like the cortizone with vanilla vodka and coffee liqueur. It is the perfect hole in the wall neighborhood bar. Nothing but locals and cheap beers around $3.
Daily 1 p.m.–4 a.m.	212-677-3160 www.karmanyc.com	They have a nice selection of flavored hookahs. It is one of the few places in the city where cigarette smoking is still allowed. Bring your friends and hang for the evening. I always get the hummus.
Daily 11 a.m.–4 a.m.	212-682-5490 www.keatskaraoke.com	A mix of an Irish Pub and a great karaoke bar. Get ready to sing because the crowd will cheer you on. My pick for a laid back karaoke experience. The menu includes all the pub food you desire.

WHAT	DEAL	LOCATION
168 **Keens** Steakhouse	Daily $6–7 bottles 5 p.m.–7 p.m. Monday–Friday FREE appetizers like wings & shrimp	72 West 36th Street (between 5th & 6th Avenues) 34 St–Herald Sq (B, D, F, M, N, Q, R) 34 St–Penn Station (1, 2, 3) 42 St–Bryant Pk (B, D, F, M) EMPIRE STATE BUILDING
Wine and spirits tastings		
169 **Kefi Restaurant** Greek Restaurant	5 p.m.–7 p.m. daily $3 wine $4 drafts $7 cocktails	505 Columbus Avenue (between 84th & 85th Streets) 86 St (A, B, C, 1, 2) 81 St–Museum of Natural History (A, B, C) UPPER WEST SIDE
Greek wine list, weekend brunch		
170 **Kennedy's** Irish Pub	5 p.m.–7 p.m. Monday–Friday $3 drafts $5 wine & well	327 West 57th Street (between 8th & 9th Avenues) 59 St–Columbus Circle (1, 2, A, B, C, D) 57 St–7 Av (N, Q, R) 7 Av (B, D, E) HELL'S KITCHEN/ MIDTOWN WEST
Sports specials, dinner specials, fireplace		

122

HOURS	CONTACT	365 EXTRAS
Mon–Fri 12 p.m.– 10:30 p.m. Sat 5 p.m.– 10:30 p.m. Sun 5 p.m.–9 p.m.	212-947-3636 www.keens.com	This place is an up-scale, classic New York Steakhouse. Think white table-cloths, dark wood and manly conver-sations. Enjoy the pub menu and happy hour special to keep things more afford-able.
Mon 5 p.m.–10 p.m. Tue–Sat 12 p.m.–11 p.m. Sun 11 a.m.–10 p.m.	212-873-0200 www.kefirestaurant. com	The sheep's milk dumplings are heav-enly. I love that the menu is reasonable and the food consis-tently outstanding. Definitely make a res-ervation or wait, it's very worth it!
Mon–Sat 11 a.m.–4 a.m. Sun 12 p.m.–4 a.m.	212-759-4242 www.kennedysny. com	You'll think you're in Ireland when you step through the door. Classic Irish menu in a warm set-ting complete with a fireplace. Jazz brunch on Sundays from 1 p.m.–3 p.m.

	WHAT	DEAL	LOCATION
171	**Keybar** Bar	4 p.m.–Close Sunday–Monday, 4 p.m.–10 p.m. Tuesday–Saturday Buy-1-get-1-FREE well, shots, cocktails, martinis, wine, import drafts & bottles	432 East 13th Street (between 1st Avenue & Avenue A) 1 Av (L) 3 Av (L) Astor Pl (4, 6, 6X) EAST VILLAGE
	FREE shots on your birthday		
172	**Killarney Rose** Bar	Daily $4 Coors pints $6 ½ yard of beer $7 ½ yard of premium beer	127 Pearl Street (between Wall Street & Hanover Square) Wall St (2, 3, 4, 5) Broad St (J, Z) FINANCIAL DISTRICT
	Sports specials		
173	**Kinsale Tavern** Irish Pub	Until 7 p.m. Monday–Friday $3.50 well & bottles $4 pints daily	1672 Third Avenue (between 93rd & 94th Streets) 96 St (4, 6, 6X) 86 St (4, 5, 6, 6X) 103 St (4, 6, 6X) UPPER EAST SIDE
124	Carries all sports including rugby and soccer		

HOURS	CONTACT	365 EXTRAS
Daily 4 p.m.–4 a.m.	212-478-3021 www.keybar.com	Get a FREE round of shots for you and your friends on your birthday (within three days). It feels like a basement with mis-matched furniture and an eclectic vibe. Love it.
Mon–Tue 11 a.m.–2 a.m. Wed–Fri 11 a.m.–4 a.m. Sat 11 a.m.–2 a.m. Sun 12 p.m.–8 p.m.	212-422-1486 www.killarneyrose.com	Classic Irish bar downstairs with lounge seating up-stairs. Good filet mignon and short-rib sliders. It's a neigh-borhood bar that always has a nice mix of people in the Wall Street area.
Daily 8 a.m.–4 a.m.	212-348-4370 www.kinsale.com	They take sports se-riously! Great prices, lots of TVs and an Irish vibe. With thirty beers on tap and a large whiskey menu, it's perfect for game day and group par-ties.

WHAT	DEAL	LOCATION
174 **Klong** Thai Restaurant	5 p.m.–7 p.m. Sunday–Thursday, 11:30 p.m.–2 a.m. Friday–Saturday, 5 p.m.–11:30 p.m. Tuesdays ½ off Singha $5–6 cocktails	7 Saint Marks Place (between 2nd & 3rd Avenues) Astor Pl (4, 6, 6X) 8 St–Nyu (N, R) 3 Av (L) EAST VILLAGE

$3–$5 appetizers

WHAT	DEAL	LOCATION
175 **K-One/KTV** Karaoke & Chinese Restaurant	Before 7 p.m. Sunday– Thursday $6 cover charge includes $6 in FREE drinks or food	97 Bowery (between Hester & Grand Street) Grand St (B, D) Bowery (J) Canal St (J, N, Q, Z) CHINATOWN

Four floors of karaoke heaven

WHAT	DEAL	LOCATION
176 **L'asso** Italian Restaurant & Pizza (2 locations)	4 p.m.–7 p.m. Monday–Friday $7 beer & 2 regular slices	192 Mott Street (at Kenmare Street) Bowery (J) Spring St (4, 6, 6X) Grand St (B, D) LITTLE ITALY

126 $20 salad and pizza lunch for two, Monday-Friday 11:30 a.m.–4 p.m.

HOURS	CONTACT	365 EXTRAS
Sun–Thu 11:30 a.m.–12 a.m. Fri–Sat 11:30 a.m.–2 a.m.	212-505-9955	The food is authentic with a modern flair. Try the pad thai and the shrimp dumplings. I am a sucker for good curries and this reasonably priced menu leaves me wanting more!
Daily 2 p.m.–4 a.m.	212-925-1999 www.konektv.com	One of the best karaoke bars in Chinatown because of it's large selection of Chinese pop songs. Definitely consider this spot for a party. There is a full service restaurant on the first floor if you're not ready to sing.
Mon–Sat 11:30 a.m.–11:30 p.m. Sun 11:30 a.m.–12:30 a.m.	212-219-2353 www.lassonyc.com	Are you a pizza snob? They offer fresh local ingredients and thin crispy crust from their wood burning oven. Try their signature D.O.C. margherita pie first then choose from more than a dozen different pizza choices.

	WHAT	DEAL	LOCATION
176	**L'asso** Italian Restaurant & Pizza (2 locations)	6 p.m.–9 p.m. Monday–Friday $5 beer & 2 regular slices	107 First Avenue (between 6th & 7th Streets) 2 Av (F) Astor Pl (4, 6, 6X) 1 Av (L) EAST VILLAGE
	$20 salad and pizza lunch for two, Monday-Friday 11:30 a.m.-4 p.m.		
177	**La Biblioteca** Mexican Restaurant & Tequila Bar	5 p.m.–8 p.m. Monday–Friday $5 beer $5 appetizers $6 wine & cocktails	622 Third Avenue, downstairs (at 40th Street) Grand Central–42 St (4, 5, 6, 6X, 7, 7X, S) GRAND CENTRAL/ MURRAY HILL
	Four hundred tequilas, private parties		
178	**La Caverna** Lounge	5 p.m.–9 p.m. daily $4 beer, wine, well	122–124 Rivington Street (between Essex & Norfolk Streets) Delancey St (F) Essex St (J, M, Z) 2 Av (F) LOWER EAST SIDE
	DJ 11 p.m.–4 a.m.		

HOURS	CONTACT	365 EXTRAS
Daily 11:30 a.m.– 11:30 p.m.	212-837-2048 www.lassonyc.com	Are you a pizza snob? They offer fresh local ingredients and thin crispy crust from their wood burning oven. Try their signature D.O.C. margherita pie first then choose from more than a dozen different pizza choices.
Mon–Wed 11:30 a.m.– 12 a.m.

Thu–Sat 11:30 a.m. – 1 a.m. | 212-808-8110 www.richardsandoval.com/labiblioteca | If you like tequilas, look no further with this enormous list. Very swanky lounge, tasty tacos and delicious drinks, oh, and did I mention the tequila? It is located downstairs from Zengo. Mingle with the beautiful people. |
| | | |
| Tue–Wed, Sun 5 p.m.–1 a.m.

Thu–Sat 5 p.m.–4 a.m. | 212-475-2126 www.lacavernanyc.com | Very cool cave like feel with modern furniture. Quite a combo! The reasonable small plate menu starts at $6. Great for parties and dancing the night away. An uncommon bar experience. |
| | | |

WHAT	DEAL	LOCATION
179 **La Linea** Bar & Lounge	Until 9 p.m. daily 11 p.m.–Close Sunday–Wednesday ½ price bar	15 First Avenue (between East Houston & 2nd Avenue) 2 Av (F) Delancey St (F) Bowery (J) EAST VILLAGE
DJ Fridays and Saturdays		
180 **Langans** Irish Pub	Daily $5 drafts Sunday & Monday nights ½ price bottles of wine $.50 wings	150 West 47th Street (between 6th & 7th Avenues) 49 St (N, Q, R) 47–50 Sts–Rockefeller Ctr (B, D, F, M) 50 St (1, 2) TIMES SQUARE/ THEATER DISTRICT
Bring ten people in on Wednesdays and get a FREE appetizer platter.		
181 **Lansdowne Road** Irish Pub	5 p.m.–7 p.m. Monday–Friday ½ Price Drinks, $5 "Daily Double" 20 ounce draft or 12 ounce bottle of beer special; Monday $.50 wings (6 piece minimum); Tuesday ½ off Irish whiskey	599 Tenth Avenue (between 43rd & 44th Streets) 42 St–Port Authority Bus Terminal (A, C, E) 50 St (A, C, E) HELL'S KITCHEN/ MIDTOWN WEST
130 FREE twenty ounce light draft or soda with sandwich Monday–Friday 12 p.m.–3 p.m.		

MONICA DINATALE

HOURS	CONTACT	365 EXTRAS
Mon–Wed, Sun 3 p.m.–3 a.m. Thu–Sat 3 p.m.–4 a.m.	212-777-1571 www.lalinealounge.com	I like the loungey low-lit vibe during the week. If you are looking for R&B classic music on weekends, definitely check them out. The bar transforms into a rowdy dance floor.
Mon–Sat 11:30 a.m.–4 a.m. Sun 12 p.m.–4 a.m.	212-869-5482 www.langans.com	Cool Irish Pub near Times Square and Rock Center. They show all sports including soccer and look great during the holidays (eggnog shots too!) FREE live music Friday–Saturday. Nice for family dinners or drinks at the bar.
Mon–Sat 11:30 a.m.–4 a.m. Sun 12 p.m.–4 a.m.	212-239-8020 www.lansdown-eroadnyc.com	You can order wings until 3 a.m. and they have fifteen beers on tap. They promote all the big games and have an excellent bar food menu. I go for the boneless chicken tenders.

WHAT	DEAL	LOCATION
182 **Latitude Bar & Grill** Bar & Grill	Until 8 p.m. Monday–Friday, Until 10 p.m. Saturday, Sunday all day $4 Bud, Bud Light, Coors Light $5 margaritas, Cosmos & martinis	783 Eighth Avenue (between 47th & 48th Streets) 50 St (A, C, E, 1, 2) 49 St (N, Q, R) TIMES SQUARE/ THEATER DISTRICT
Twenty HD TVs, comedy, pool table, karaoke, DJs		
183 **Legends** Sports Bar	4 p.m.–7 p.m. Monday–Friday $4 drafts $6 wine & well	6 West 33rd Street (between 5th & 6th Avenues) 34 St–Herald Sq (B, D, F, M, N, Q, R) 28 St (N, R) 33 St (4, 6, 6X) EMPIRE STATE BUILDING
If you bring a group of ten people, you'll get FREE drinks on your birthday.		
184 **Lenox Lounge** Bar/Restaurant & Live Jazz	5 p.m.–7 p.m. Monday–Friday $3 domestic beer $5 specialty cocktails	330 Lenox Avenue (between 124th & 125th Streets) 125 St (2, 3, A, B, C, D) 116 St (2, 3) HARLEM
Check website for jazz schedule.		

HOURS	CONTACT	365 EXTRAS
Mon–Tue 3 p.m.–2 a.m. Wed–Fri 3 p.m.–4 a.m. Sat 12 p.m.–4 a.m. Sun 12 p.m.–2 a.m.	212-245-3034 www.latitudebarnyc.com	An enormous up-scale bar with three floors and rooftop to choose from. Try the Philly cheese steak spring rolls and the black truffle fries. Great prices close to Times Square.
Daily 11 a.m.–4 a.m.	212-967-7792 www.legends33.com	Twenty plus beers on tap and classic bar food menu. Absolutely perfect for watching sporting events. Check out the "football factory" room for all inclusive specials during big games.
Daily 12 p.m.–4 a.m.	212-427-0253 www.lenoxlounge.com	The classic Harlem jazz club with tons of history. The original location was a few doors down but this location keeps the good vibes. It's amazing to see talented musicians with covers from $10–$20. No cover for bar seating.

	WHAT	DEAL	LOCATION
185	**Lilly O'Brien's** Irish Pub	4 p.m.–8 p.m. Monday–Friday $1 off drafts $3.50 bottles $4.50 well	67 Murray Street (between West Broadway & Greenwich Streets) Chambers St (1, 2, 3, A, C) Park Pl (2, 3) TRIBECA
	Fourteen HD TVs, sports specials		
186	**Lincoln Park Grill** Bar & Grill	Daily $3 Bud & Bud Light $3 PBR tallboys	867 Ninth Avenue (between 56th & 57th Streets) 59 St–Columbus Circle (1, 2, A, B, C, D) 57 St–7 Av (N, Q, R) 50 St (A, C, E) HELL'S KITCHEN/ MIDTOWN WEST
	$12 weekend brunch includes one FREE mimosa, screwdriver or Bloody Mary.		
187	**Lion's Head Tavern** Bar & Restaurant	Daily $2.50 PBR 5 p.m.–8 p.m. Monday–Friday $1 off drafts & well $2 off pitchers	995 Amsterdam Avenue (between 108th & 109th Streets) Cathedral Pkwy (110 St) (1, A, B, C) UPPER WEST SIDE
	Daily drink specials, sports specials		

MONICA DiNATALE

HOURS	CONTACT	365 EXTRAS
Mon–Wed, Sun 10 a.m.–2 a.m. Thu–Sat 10 a.m.–4 a.m.	212-732-1592 www.lillyobriensbar.com	The "bartenders know your name" type of place. Check them out if you're a soccer fan. Large party room downstairs, thirteen beers on tap and a pub menu including Irish favorites.
Daily 12 p.m.–4 a.m.	212-974-2826 www.lpgnyc.com	The $3 PBR tallboys make this a popular beer bar. Expect lots of drink specials. The classic pub style appetizer menu is perfect for sharing. I'm a fan of the chicken fingers.
Mon–Fri 5 p.m.–4 a.m. Sat–Sun 12 p.m.–4 a.m.	212-866-1030	In the Columbia area, so filled with either students or locals. Where else can you find tater tots on the menu? It's a fun place with reasonable options and great deals every day.

188

| Locksmith Wine Bar
 Wine Bar | 3 p.m.–8 p.m. daily

 $3 beer & well | 4463 Broadway
 (between Fairview Avenue & 192nd Street)
 190 St (A)
 191 St (1)
 Dyckman St (1)

 WASHINGTON HEIGHTS |

Weekend brunch includes one FREE beverage.

189

| Lolita
 Bar | 5 p.m.–8 p.m. daily

 $3 drafts
 $4 well | 266 Broome Street
 (between Allen & Orchard Streets)
 Delancey St (F)
 Essex St (J, M, Z)
 Grand St (B, D)

 LOWER EAST SIDE |

Comedy shows, cash and American Express® only

190

| Loreley
 German Restaurant & Biergarten | 5 p.m.–7 p.m. Sunday–Thursday

 $2 off drafts, wine & well | 7 Rivington Street
 (between Chrystie & Bowery Streets)
 Grand St (B, D)
 Bowery (J)
 2 Av (F)

 LOWER EAST SIDE |

Outdoor seating, brunch daily

MONICA DiNATALE

HOURS	CONTACT	365 EXTRAS
Mon–Wed 3 p.m.–2 a.m. Thu–Fri 3 p.m.–4 a.m. Sat–Sun 12 p.m.–4 a.m.	212-304-9463	It's vibe is cantina with a nice wine list and good burgers. Delicous wings and garlic or yucca fries. It's small and can get packed on weekends so get there early for your best shot at scoring a seat.
Daily 5 p.m.–4 a.m.	212-966-7223 www.lolitabar.net	It has that artsy Lower East Side feel. So comfy you won't want to leave. Get there early for a seat on the couches in the back. No food menu. A real gem.
Mon–Tue, Sun 12 p.m.–1 a.m. Wed 12 p.m.–2 a.m. Thu 12 p.m.–3 a.m. Fri–Sat 12 p.m.–4 a.m.	212-253-7077 www.loreleynyc.com	Twelve German beers on tap and an authentic menu including a large array of wurst and schnitzel. There is a small outdoor area. Get a pretzel now and enjoy!

| **191** **Lucky Strike Bowling** Restaurant & Bowling | 5 p.m.–8 p.m. & 10 p.m.–12 a.m. Monday–Friday ½ price well & domestic beer | 650 West 42nd Street (between 11th & 12th Streets) 42 St–Times Sq (1, 9, 2, A, C, E) HELL'S KITCHEN/ MIDTOWN WEST |

Bowling parties with many options

| **192** **Lucky Strike** American/French Restaurant & Bar | 4 p.m.–7 p.m. daily $4 Yuengling ½ price wine & well $5 appetizers like calamari & mini burgers | 59 Grand Street (between Wooster & West Broadway) Canal St (1, 2, A, C, E, N, R) SOHO |

Prix-fixe menus

| **193** **Lure Fishbar** Seafood Restaurant | 5 p.m.–7 p.m. Monday–Friday $1–$1.50 clams & oysters $5 beer $7 wine $8 specialty cocktails | 142 Mercer Street (at Prince Street) Prince St (N, R) Broadway–Lafayette St (B, D, F, M) Spring St (4, 6, 6X) SOHO |

Outstanding raw bar, weekend brunch

MONICA DiNATALE

HOURS	CONTACT	365 EXTRAS
Mon–Thu, Sun 12 p.m.–2 a.m. Fri–Sat 12 p.m.–4 a.m.	646-829-0170 www.bowl-luckystrike.com	Huge, modern and sleek bowling lounge. Good food, scene, drinks, and fun—this is not the bowling lane you grew up with. It's a combination of night club and bowling alley.
Mon–Wed, Sun 12 p.m.–1 a.m. Thu 12 p.m.–2 a.m. Fri–Sat 12 p.m.– 2:30 a.m.	212-941-0772 www.luckystrikeny.com	Think intimate French bistro with great steak frites. The menu offers something for everyone making it a nice place for dinner and/or drinks with friends. Hello, date night.
Mon–Thu 11:30 a.m.– 11 p.m. Fri 11:30 a.m.– 12 a.m. Sat 5 p.m.–12 a.m.	212-431-7676 www.lurefishbar.com	You will definitely think you are in the bow of a cruise ship as you enter. Very cool ship-like décor and delicious upscale seafood. My favorite is the yellowtail carpaccio.

	WHAT	DEAL	LOCATION
194	**M1-5** Club & Restaurant	4 p.m.–12 a.m. Monday–Wednesday, 4 p.m.–10 p.m. Thursday–Friday, 8 p.m.–10 p.m. Saturday, Sunday all day during sports ½ price beer, wine, well $2 off top shelf	52 Walker Street (between Church Street & Broadway) Canal St (A, C, E, N, R, 4, 6, 6X) TRIBECA
	Food specials, sports specials		
195	**Mad Dogs & Beans** Mexican Cantina	2 p.m.– 5:30 p.m. Monday–Friday Buy-1-get-1- FREE drinks ½ price guacamole	83 Pearl Street (between Broad & William Streets) Whitehall St (N, R) Broad St (J, Z) Wall St (2, 3) FINANCIAL DISTRICT
	Dinner specials Monday–Friday 5 p.m.–11 p.m., $15 brunch Saturday and Sunday 11:30 a.m.–4 p.m.		
196	**Mad River Bar & Grille** Bar & Restaurant	Sunday sports specials; Tuesday $4 beer & specialty drinks 8p.m.–10 p.m.; Wednesday ½ off la- dies; Thursday $2–$5 beer & shots 7 p.m.–12 a.m.; Friday VIP Happy Hour $10 at the door for $2 drafts and $3 well 7 p.m.–10 p.m.	1442 Third Avenue (at 82nd Street) 86 St (4, 5, 6, 6X) 77 St (4, 6, 6X) UPPER EAST SIDE
	Fifteen HD TVs, sports specials, private room		

MONICA DiNATALE

HOURS	CONTACT	365 EXTRAS
Mon–Fri 4 p.m.–4 a.m. Sat 8 p.m.–4 a.m.	212-965-1701 www.M1-5.com	A large, exciting club for dancing, drinking, late night deals, and later nights. $30 brunch with unlimited drinks on weekends until 4 p.m. You won't find "bottle service" prices here, just a good time.
Mon–Fri 11:30 a.m.–11:30 p.m. Sat–Sun 12 p.m.–10 p.m.	212-269-1177 www.maddogand-beans.com	I love fresh guacamole. Try the queso fundito and the mahi-mahi tacos. In nice weather sit outside and be prepared to sip the day away and watch the world go by.
Daily 11 a.m.–4 a.m.	212-988-1832 www.madrivergrille.com	It has a very upbeat Mexican atmosphere. They offer Tuesday trivia, and always have special events going on. Tons of food and drink specials every day, including $6 for eight wings during sporting events.

	WHAT	DEAL	LOCATION
197	**Mamajuana Café** Mexican Cantina	4 p.m.–12 a.m. Monday, 4 p.m.–7 p.m. Tuesday–Thursday Buy-1-get-1-FREE drinks	247 Dyckman Street (between Seaman & Payson Street) Dyckman St (1, A) Inwood–207 St (A) INWOOD
	Check website for live music schedule, dancing & seasonal drink specials. (new location on UPPER WEST SIDE)		
198	**Manhattan Brewhouse** Bar & Restaurant	4 p.m.–7 p.m. Monday–Friday $5 beer $6 appetizers & well $7 wine & cocktails $15 appetizer towers	354 Third Avenue (at 26th Street) 23 St, 28 St, 33 St (4, 6, 6X) FLATIRON/GRAMERCY
	$14.95 brunch on weekends includes one FREE beverage.		
199	**Manny's On Second** Sports Bar	4 p.m.–7 p.m. Monday–Friday ½ price beer, wine & well	1770 Second Avenue (between 92nd & 93rd Streets) 96 St (4, 6, 6X) 86 St (4, 5, 6, 6X) UPPER EAST SIDE
142	Twenty four beers on tap, forty HD TVs		

HOURS	CONTACT	365 EXTRAS
Daily 6 p.m.–12 a.m.	212-304-0140 www.mamajua-nacafenyc.com	Try the sangria and a ceviche. It's the perfect combination! The dining room is very large with a cool terra cotta vibe. They always have FREE entertainment going on.
Daily 11 a.m.–4 a.m.	212-696-1011 www.manhattanbre-whouse.com	Airy sports bar and restaurant with craft beers and a great selection of appetizers. Check the website for visiting DJs and special events like trivia nights. $10 lunch specials 12 p.m.– 4 p.m. weekdays.
Mon–Wed, Sun 11:30 a.m.– 2 a.m. Thu–Sat 11:30 a.m.– 4 a.m.	212-410-3300 www.mannysonsec-ond.com	A sports lover's paradise with TVs in every corner so you never miss a minute of the action. If that's not enough, checkers, Trivial Pursuit® and Jenga® will keep you busy. Perfect for any sporting event.

WHAT	DEAL	LOCATION
Maya Mexican Restaurant	5 p.m.–8 p.m. Tuesday–Saturday, Sunday & Monday all night $4 beers $6 margaritas, sangria & wine 5 p.m.–10 p.m. Tuesday $5 tacos	1191 First Avenue (between 64th & 65th Streets) Lexington Av/59 St (F, N, Q, R) 68 St–Hunter College (4, 6, 6X) UPPER EAST SIDE
Tequila menu and tastings		
McAleer's Pub & Restaurant Irish Pub	Until 5 p.m. Monday–Friday ½ price drafts	425 Amsterdam Avenue (between 80th & 81st Streets) 79 St (1, 2) 86 St (1, 2) 81 St–Museum of Natural History (A, B, C) UPPER WEST SIDE
Beer, shot and wing specials		
McCormick & Schmick's Seafood Restaurant & Bar	3:30 p.m.–7 p.m. Monday–Friday, 3 p.m.–5 p.m. Saturday $4–5 drafts $5 wine $4–$6 appetizers	1285 Avenue of the Americas, on 52nd Street (between 6th & 7th Avenues) 7 Av (B, D, E) 50 St (1, 2) 47–50 Sts–Rockefeller Ctr (B, D, F, M) RADIO CITY/ ROCKEFELLER CENTER
Try the $4 cheese burger and fries from 3:30 p.m.–7 p.m.		

200
201
202

MONICA DiNATALE

HOURS	CONTACT	365 EXTRAS
Mon–Thu, Sun 5 p.m.–10 p.m. Fri–Sat 5 p.m.–11 p.m.	212-585-1818 www.richardsandoval.com/mayany/index.php	Authentic homemade Mexican food and a huge tequila list. Try the Atlantic cod tacos or the huitlacoche enchiladas. The menu is upscale making the deals even sweeter. Modern and sexy.
Daily 11 a.m.–4 a.m.	212-362-7867 www.mcaleerspub.com	I like the burgers and can't get enough of the nachos. It's a fun place to watch sports or enjoy the sidewalk seating in warmer weather. It's extremely comfortable and inviting.
Mon–Sat 11:30 a.m.–11 p.m. Sun 12 p.m.–10 p.m.	212-459-1222 www.mccormickandschmicks.com	This place has that classic Midtown upscale vibe. Great spot for a power lunch. Take advantage of the specials for a real deal! If you want to splurge, go for the seared yellowfin ahi tuna.

	WHAT	DEAL	LOCATION
203	**McCoy's Bar** Bar	10 a.m.–7 p.m. daily $4 beers $5 well, Cosmos & shots Add $1 after 7 p.m.–Close	768 Ninth Avenue (between 51st & 52nd Streets) 50 St (1, 2, A, C, E) 7 Av (B, D, E) HELL'S KITCHEN/MIDTOWN WEST
	Drink specials, sports specials, eleven HD TVs		
204	**McFadden's** Bar & Restaurant	6 p.m.–9 p.m. Monday–Friday ½ price drinks 6 p.m.–12 a.m. Monday $3 drafts & ½ price appetizers Tuesday $1 drafts	800 Second Avenue (between 42nd & 43rd Streets) Grand Central–42 St (4, 5, 6, 6X, 7, 7X, S) GRAND CENTRAL
	Check the website for new discounted events every week.		
205	**McKenna's Pub** Bar & Restaurant	12 p.m.–7 p.m. daily Buy-1-get-1-FREE drinks	250 West 14th Street (between 7th & 8th Avenues) 8 Av (L) 14 St (A, C, E, 1, 2, 3) THE VILLAGE
	Sports specials		

MONICA DiNATALE

HOURS	CONTACT	365 EXTRAS
Daily 10 a.m.–4 a.m.	212-957-8055 www.mccoysbarnyc.com	I like this place because it's small and cozy off the bustle of Ninth Avenue. The booths are nice in the back and the burgers are always satisfying. They have fifteen beers on tap including Guinness.
Daily 11 a.m.–4 a.m.	212-986-1515 www.mcfaddens42.com	There is always a large crowd having fun at this Midtown gem. A friendly spot to make new friends. Lots of specials every day and $1 drafts on Tuesdays!
Daily 11 a.m.–4 a.m.	212-255-2889	Reasonable food menu and cheap drinks every day. A friendly staff, couches, Christmas lights and a relaxed vibe. A nice spot for a lazy afternoon.

WHAT	DEAL	LOCATION
206 **McSorley's Old Ale House** Bar	Daily $5.50 for 2 beers	15 East 7th Street (between Cooper Square & Taras Shevchenko Place) Astor Pl (4, 6, 6X) 8 St–Nyu (N, R) Bleecker St (4, 6, 6X) EAST VILLAGE
They make their own beer and that's it!		
207 **Meade's Bar** Bar & Restaurant	4 p.m.–6 p.m. Monday–Friday $2 beer $4 well $5 mini-appetizers $12 ½ wine carafe $14 quart margaritas	22 Peck Slip (at Water Street) Fulton St (A, C, J, Z, 2, 3) Brooklyn Bridge–City Hall (4, 5, 6, 6X) SOUTH STREET SEAPORT
Weekend brunch with unlimited drinks		
208 **Mercadito** Mexican Restaurant (2 locations)	4 p.m.–6:30 p.m. Monday–Friday ½ price margaritas & guacamole	100 Seventh Avenue South (at Grove Street) Christopher St–Sheridan Sq (1, 2) W 4 St (A, B, C, D, E, F, M) Houston St (1, 2) THE VILLAGE
$18 weekend brunch includes one FREE drink.		

HOURS	CONTACT	365 EXTRAS
Mon–Sat 11 a.m.–1 a.m. Sun 1 p.m.–1 a.m.	212-473-9148 www.mcsorleysn-ewyork.com	The oldest continuously operating saloon in New York City. You order light (color), dark, or light and dark. Ordering "light and dark beers for four" will yield eight draft mugs. Communal seating takes me back in time. Go!
Mon–Sun 12 p.m.–12 a.m. Tue–Sat 12 p.m.–2 a.m.	212-791-1818 www.meadespub. com	Being at the Seaport makes me feel like I'm visiting a fishing village not roaming New York City! This place is a casual and inviting oasis after a hard days work. You will always find drink specials.
Mon–Wed 3 p.m.–11 p.m. Thu–Fri 3 p.m.–12 a.m. Sat–Sun 12 p.m.–4 a.m. Sat 5 p.m.–12 a.m. Sun 5 p.m.–11 p.m.	212-647-0830 www.mercaditor-estaurants.com	Outstanding authentic Mexican restaurants that are cozy and delicious. Their guacamole often incorporates interesting seasonal flavors like mango or chipotle. Order the "three guacamoles" to taste more than one!

	WHAT	DEAL	LOCATION
208	**Mercadito** Mexican Restaurant (2 locations)	5 p.m.–6:30 p.m. Monday–Friday $5 margaritas & guacamole	179 Avenue B (between 11th & 12th Streets) 1 Av (L) EAST VILLAGE
	$18 weekend brunch includes one FREE drink.		
209	**Mercury Bar** Bar & Restaurant	4 p.m.–8 p.m. daily $4 drafts & shots $5 wine, specialty cocktails & frozen drinks $5 appetizers $15 beer buckets (5) $20 margarita & sangria pitchers	659 Ninth Avenue (between 45th & 46th Streets) 42 St–Port Authority Bus Terminal (A, C, E) 50 St (A, C, E) 49 St (N, Q, R) HELL'S KITCHEN/ MIDTOWN WEST
	Nine TVs, sports specials		
210	**Merrion** Bar & Restaurant	Daily FREE order of wings with pitcher purchased (except Yuengling), FREE Merrion burger with full-price drink Open–7 p.m. Monday–Friday $3–$4 drafts & bottles $4 well & wine	1840 Second Avenue (at 95th Street) 96 St (4, 6, 6X) 103 St (4, 6, 6X) UPPER EAST SIDE
	Pool table, Philadelphia sports teams bar		

HOURS	CONTACT	365 EXTRAS
Mon–Tue, Sun 5 p.m.–11 p.m. Wed–Thu 5 p.m.–12 a.m. Fri–Sat 5 p.m.–1 a.m. Sat–Sun 12 p.m.–4 a.m.	718-535-7984 www.mercaditor-estaurants.com	Outstanding authentic Mexican restaurants that are cozy and delicious. Their guacamole often incorporates interesting seasonal flavors like mango or chipotle. Order the "three guacamoles" to taste more than one!
Mon–Fri 11 a.m.–4 a.m. Sat–Sun 10 a.m.–4 a.m.	212-262-7755 www.mercuryba-rnyc.com	A large bar with plenty of TVs and solid food. The menu offers everything from burgers to spaghetti and meatballs. There is always a nice crowd and a special going on. Popular for sports on weekends.
Mon–Tue 5 p.m.–4 a.m. Wed–Sun 12 p.m.–4 a.m.	212-831-7696 www.merrionnyc.com	This sports bar attracts Philadelphia Eagles and Phillies fans in season. The FREE burgers are about ⅓ pound and really delicious considering the price! Sixteen beers on tap and TVs in every corner.

	WHAT	DEAL	LOCATION
211	**Milano's Bar** Bar	4 p.m.–7 p.m. Monday–Friday $1 off all drinks $6 Rolling Rock & shot	51 East Houston Street (between Mott & Mulberry Streets) Bleecker St (4, 6, 6X) Broadway–Lafayette St (B, D, F, M) Prince St (N, R) LITTLE ITALY
	Jukebox		
212	**Moca Lounge** Lounge	5 p.m.–9 p.m. Monday– Thursday, 5 p.m.–8 p.m. Saturday– Sunday ½ price beer & well	2210 Frederick Douglas Boulevard (between 119th & 120th Streets) 116 St (A, B, C, 2, 3) 125 St (A, B, C, D) HARLEM
	Food specials		
213	**Móle** Mexican Restaurant (3 locations)	4 p.m.–7 p.m. Monday–Friday, 2 p.m.–7 p.m. Saturday– Sunday $4 drafts $5 margaritas $5 quesadillas, guacamole, nachos	205 Allen Street (at Houston Street) 2 Av (F) Delancey St (F) Bowery (J) LOWER EAST SIDE
	Homemade guacamole and Mexican favorites		

HOURS	CONTACT	365 EXTRAS
Mon–Sat 8 a.m.–4 a.m. Sun 12 p.m.–4 a.m.	212-226-8844	This is a perfectly friendly small dive bar with a rock n' roll jukebox. Low key and unpretentious with cheap drinks. Seems like people have been sitting there for years...
Mon–Tue 5 p.m.–2 a.m. Wed–Thu, Sun 1 p.m.–2 a.m. Fri–Sat 11 a.m.–4 a.m.	212-665-8081	Small local find with a nice American menu and comfortable seating. If I had a bar in my home, I would design it like this place. Hip-hop, Motown classics and R&B music keep the place lively.
Sun–Thu 12 p.m.–11 p.m. Fri–Sat 12 p.m.–12 a.m.	212-777-3200 www.molenyc.com	Try the fish tacos and the guacamole made table side. They only take reservations for six or more but it's worth the wait. Large portions and strong margaritas, what more do you need?

	WHAT	DEAL	LOCATION
213	**Móle** Mexican Restaurant **(3 locations)**	4 p.m.–7p.m. daily $5 drafts $6 margaritas $5 quesadillas, guacamole, nachos	57 Jane Street **(at Hudson Street)** **8 Av (L)** **14 St (A, C, E, 1, 2, 3)** THE VILLAGE
	Homemade guacamole and Mexican favorites		
213	**Móle** Mexican Restaurant **(3 locations)**	4 p.m.–7 p.m. daily $4 drafts $5 margaritas $5 quesadillas, guacamole, nachos	1735 Second Avenue **(between 89th & 90th Streets)** **86 St (4, 5, 6, 6X)** **96 St (4, 6, 6X)** UPPER EAST SIDE
214	**Molly Pitcher's Ale House** Irish Pub	11 a.m.–7 p.m. Monday–Friday $3 domestic drafts & bottles $4 well & beer $5 martinis	1641 Second Avenue **(at 85th Street)** **86 St (4, 5, 6, 6X)** **77 St (4, 6, 6X)** UPPER EAST SIDE
154	Twelve HD TVs		

HOURS	CONTACT	365 EXTRAS
Sun–Thu 12 p.m.–11 p.m. Fri–Sat 12 p.m.–12 a.m.	212-206-7577 www.molenyc.com	Try the fish tacos and the guacamole made table side. They only take reservations for six or more but it's worth the wait. Large portions and strong margaritas, what more do you need?
Sun–Thu 12 p.m.–11 p.m. Fri–Sat 12 p.m.–12 a.m.	212-289-8226 www.molenyc.com	
Daily 11 a.m.–4 a.m.	212-249-3067 www.mollypitcher-snyc.com	Irish restaurant and sports bar with classic burgers and traditional Irish fare. They love their sports specials and attract Baltimore Ravens fans during football season. Weekend brunch includes one FREE beverage.

	WHAT	DEAL	LOCATION
215	**Mother Burger** Bar & Restaurant	Daily $2 beer $3 frozen margaritas $3 frozen mojitos	329 West 49th Street (between 8th & 9th Avenues) 50 St (A, C, E, 1, 2) 49 St (N, Q, R) TIMES SQUARE/ THEATER DISTRICT
	FREE shelled peanuts, extensive outdoor seating		
216	**Mudville 9** Bar & Restaurant	Daily $4 Budweiser $5 Svedka vodka drinks $6 craft beers	126 Chambers Street (between Church Street & West Broadway) Chambers St (1, 2, 3, A, C) Park Pl (2, 3) TRIBECA
	$24.95 "Wing Ding" Special: All-you-can-eat wings and fries/unlimited pitchers for two hours (6 people)		
217	**Murphy's** Irish Pub	Daily $4 bottles $5 wine & well $15 pitchers	977 Second Avenue (between 51st & 52nd Streets) Lexington Av/53 St (E, M) 51 St (4, 6, 6X) 59 St (4, 5, 6, 6X) MIDTOWN EAST
	Jukebox		

MONICA DiNATALE

HOURS	CONTACT	365 EXTRAS
Sun–Thu 11:30 a.m.– 11 p.m. Fri–Sat 11:30 a.m.– 12 a.m.	212-757-8600 www.motherburger. com	Tasty burgers, dogs, fries and of course, beer. The bonus is it's location in World-wide Plaza that pro-vides a quiet place to sit and have drink. The complex is a unique place to avoid those busy New York streets.
Mon–Thu 10 a.m.–1 a.m. Fri–Sat 10 a.m.–2 a.m. Sun 10 a.m.–10 p.m.	212-964-9464 www.mudville9.com	Join the "beer club" for special savings. They have twenty plus beers on tap, a great staff and an excellent variety of wings. I've come here with groups of ten and always left wanting to come back.
Daily 11a.m.–4 a.m.	212-751-5400 www.mudville9.com	You know you are in for a good time when the bartenders Irish accent is so thick you can bearly under-stand what they are saying. This is a very friendly neighboor-hood pub. Bring your smile and you just may get a "buyback."

	WHAT	DEAL	LOCATION
218	**Mustang Harry's** Bar & Restaurant	3 p.m.–7 p.m. daily $2.50 PBR $4 beers & Jameson shots $5 Cosmos $5 wings	352 Seventh Avenue (between 29th & 30th Streets) 28 St (1, 2) 34 St–Penn Station (1, 2, 3, A, C, E) MADISON SQUARE GARDEN/PENN STATION
	Sports specials, comedy		
219	**Mustang Sally's** Bar & Restaurant	3 p.m.–7 p.m. Monday–Friday $4.50 drafts, shots & well $5.50 martinis	324 Seventh Avenue (between 28th & 29th Streets) 28 St (1, 2) 34 St–Penn Station (1, 2, 3) 23 St (1, 2) MADISON SQUARE GARDEN/PENN STATION
	Daily specials, private room		
220	**Nancy Whiskey Pub** Bar & Restaurant	4 p.m.–7 p.m. Monday–Thursday $2.50 Bud & Bud Light bottles and drafts $10 pitchers	1 Lispenard Street (between West Broadway and Church Street) Canal St (A, C, E, 1, 2) Franklin St (1, 2) TRIBECA
	Sports specials, shuffleboard		

HOURS	CONTACT	365 EXTRAS
Daily 11 a.m.–4 a.m.	212-268-8930 www.mustangharrys.com	Lots of booths and seating in the back make it nice for larger parties. The food is reasonably priced and includes everything from calamari and pastas to burgers and pub fare.
Mon–Sat 10 a.m.–4 a.m. Sun 11 a.m.–2 a.m.	212-695-3806 www.mustangsallysny.com	I like the chicken kebab salad and the grilled cheese with tomato. A good pick for meeting friends before visiting the Garden or stopping off en route to Penn Station.
Mon–Sat 9 a.m.–4 a.m. Sun 12 p.m.–4 a.m.	212-226-9943 www.nancywhiskeypub.com	A hidden gem of a dive bar with great happy hour prices. Shuffleboard is just perfect when enjoying a drink on a casual night. You will find mostly locals who are friendly and ready to chat.

	WHAT	DEAL	LOCATION
221	**Naples 45** Italian Restaurant	5 p.m.–7 p.m. Monday–Friday FREE Pizza	200 Park Avenue, Met Life Building (at 45th Street) Grand Central–42 St (4, 5, 6, 6X, 7, 7X, S) GRAND CENTRAL
	Wood-burning oven, outdoor seating		
222	**No Idea Bar** Bar	5 p.m.–4 a.m. daily $4 No Idea ale $6 well $7 Schaefer & Bushmills whiskey shot	30 East 20th Street (between Broadway and Park Avenue South) 23 St (4, 6, 6X, N, R) 14 St–Union Sq (N, Q, R) FLATIRON/ GRAMERCY
	FREE drinks daily for "name night" if your name is selected from 5 p.m.–11 p.m.		
223	**Nurse Bettie** Bar	6 p.m.–10 p.m. daily Sunday all day $4 drafts & well	106 Norfolk Street (between Delancey & Rivington Streets) Essex St (J, M, Z) Delancey St (F) 2 Av (F) LOWER EAST SIDE
	FREE Pizza 6:30 p.m.–8 p.m. Monday–Friday		

MONICA DiNATALE

HOURS	CONTACT	365 EXTRAS
Mon–Fri 7:30 a.m.– 10 p.m.	212-972-7001 www.naples45nyc. com	The FREE pizza is worth a visit. Beers start at $6.50 and wines $8.50. It is a very comfortable Italian restaurant that is known for excellent pizza near Grand Central.
Mon–Fri 4:30 p.m.–4 a.m. Sat 6 p.m.–4 a.m.	212-777-0100 www.noideabar.com	They make their own vodka and only carry the No Idea brand. You can order food from their "book of one thousand menus." This is a good place to meet your friends.
Daily 6 p.m.–4 a.m.	917-434-9072 www.nursebettie. com	Take a trip back in time! Inspired retro décor, pin-ups from the 1950's and live FREE burlesque on Wednesdays and Thursdays. Great specialty drinks. Only in New York.

WHAT	DEAL	LOCATION
224 **O'Flaherty's Ale House** Irish Ale House & Restaurant	4 p.m.–7 p.m. daily $3 pints, champagne & warm cocktails like hot cider & Irish toddies	334 West 46th Street (between 8th & 9th Avenues) 42 St–Port Authority Bus Terminal (A, C, E) 50 St (A, C, E) 49 St (N, Q, R) TIMES SQUARE/ THEATER DISTRICT
FREE live music daily at 10:30 p. m.		
225 **O'Flanagan's** Irish Pub	4 p.m.–7 p.m. Monday–Friday $3 bottles $3.50 drafts & well $4 flavored Stoli	1215 First Avenue (between 65th & 66th Streets) Lexington Av/63 St (F) 68 St–Hunter College (4, 6, 6X) Lexington Av/59 St (N, Q, R) UPPER EAST SIDE
Private parties, live music		
226 **O'Hara's** Irish Pub	Daily $3 Coors $5 bottles & shots $6 drafts	120 Cedar Street Suite 4 (between Greenwich Street & Trinity Place) Cortlandt St (N, R) Wall St (4, 5) Rector St (1) FINANCIAL DISTRICT
Food specials, sports specials		

MONICA DINATALE

HOURS	CONTACT	365 EXTRAS
Daily 12 p.m.–4 a.m.	212-581-9366 www.oflahertysny.com	They offer a prime location on restaurant row right in the heart of the Theater District. The whole place feels like a cluster of small dens with tons of library books and charm. In the back there is an outdoor garden.
Daily 10 a.m.–4 a.m.	212-439-0660 www.oflanagans.com	Check website for DJs, live music and karaoke schedules. They offer an impressive menu variety and carry all major sporting events. It's my pick for cheering on the New York City marathoners in November!
Daily 10:30 a.m.– 1 a.m.	212-267-3032	Welcoming Irish pub in the vicinity of 9-11 Memorial. It reminds me of an old time patriotic steel workers bar. The casual bar menu and reasonable drinks make it a perfect place to pass the time. Totally chill.

	WHAT	DEAL	LOCATION
227	**Old Town Bar** Bar & Restaurant	Daily $5 beers $6 wine $7 well	45 East 18th Street (between Broadway & Park Avenue South) 14 St–Union Sq (4, 5, 6, 6X, L, N, Q, R) FLATIRON/ GRAMERCY
	Writers love this place and many have books on the walls.		
228	**Oliver's City Tavern** Bar & Restaurant	4 p.m.–7 p.m. Monday–Friday Buy-1-get-1-FREE drafts, wine & well	190 West 4th Street (corner of Barrow Street, between 6th & 7th Avenues) Christopher St–Sheridan Sq (1, 2) W 4 St (A, B, C, D, E, F, M) Houston St (1, 2) THE VILLAGE
	$14.95 brunch includes two FREE drinks.		
229	**One and One** Irish Pub	12 p.m.–8 p.m. Monday–Friday, 12 p.m.–7 p.m. Sunday $2 off bar (except top shelf liquor); 7 p.m.–1 a.m. Sunday ½ price fish n' chips; 7 p.m.–1 a.m. Monday $.20 wings; 7 p.m.–1 a.m. Tuesday $1 sliders	76 East First Street (at 1st Avenue) 2 Av (F) Delancey St (F) Essex St (J, M, Z) EAST VILLAGE
	Fourteen rotating drafts, six HD TVs, drink specials		

HOURS	CONTACT	365 EXTRAS
Mon–Sat 11:30 a.m.– 12:30 a.m. Sun 12 p.m.–12 a.m.	212-529-6732 www.oldtownbar.com	Great history and old time New York pub décor from the 1800's. Tall ceilings, dark wood, generous pours and solid food. You'll see why it's been used for so many movies and TV shows.
Mon–Thu 12 p.m.–2 a.m. Fri 12 p.m.–4 a.m. Sat 11 a.m.–4 a.m. Sun 11 a.m.–2 a.m.	212-647-0500 www.oliverscity-tavern.com	This is the kind of bright bar that begs you to stop in and have a drink. Watch the world go by from the wall of windows. Order the fish and chips, enjoy the view and relax.
Daily 12 p.m.–4 a.m.	212-598-9126 www.oneandoneny.com	This two level pub gets a nice mixed crowd and the food is always inexpensive. You can visit Katz's Deli across the street too, come here for drinks, more food, and a good evening.

	WHAT	DEAL	LOCATION
230	**Onieal's** Bar & Restaurant	4:30 p.m.– 7 p.m. Monday–Friday $4–$6 drafts $6 well	174 Grand Street (at Baxter Street) Canal St (4, 6, 6X, J, N, Q, Z) Spring St (4, 6, 6X) LITTLE ITALY
	Used as Steve's Bar in "Sex And The City"		
231	**Opal** Bar & Restaurant	12 p.m.–7 p.m. Monday–Friday ½ price drinks Sunday $3 drafts $5 well	251 East 52nd Street (at 2nd Avenue) Lexington Av/53 St (E, M) 51 St (4, 6, 6X) 59 St (4, 5, 6, 6X) MIDTOWN EAST
	Daily food and drink specials, comedy shows		
232	**Oro Bakery & Bar** Wine Bar & French/American Restaurant	4 p.m.–8 p.m. Monday– Saturday ½ price beer, wine, saké & champagne cocktails, sangria	375 Broome Street (between Mott & Mulberry Streets) Bowery (J) Spring St (4, 6, 6X) Grand St (B, D) LITTLE ITALY
	Special occasion and wedding cakes		

HOURS	CONTACT	365 EXTRAS
Mon–Thu, Sun 11:30 a.m.–2 a.m. Fri–Sat 11:30 a.m.–4 a.m.	212-941-9119 www.onieals.com	If you've tired of Italian food in Little Italy, try a burger. I like to sit in the lounge area with couch seating. The menu changes with the seasons and they offer interesting cocktails. Late night menu too!
Daily 11 a.m.–4 a.m.	212-593-4321 www.opalbar.com	They blend a contemporary vibe in a beer bar setting. Great for drinks and conversation. I like that there are several bottles of wine under $40 and that they offer an all day brunch for $11-$15.
Mon 7 a.m.–12 a.m. Tue–Wed 7 a.m.–1 a.m. Thu–Sat 7 a.m.–2 a.m. Sun 8 a.m.–12 a.m.	212-941-6368 www.orobakerybar.com	Wine bar and café with organic wines, beers and sakes. It's a combination coffee bar, patisserie and neighborhood lounge. Try any of the homemade pastries, scones or muffins. Small and casual.

WHAT	DEAL	LOCATION
233 **Overlook** Bar & Restaurant	2 p.m.–6 p.m. Monday–Friday 2-for-1 drinks	225 East 44th Street **(between 2nd & 3rd Avenues) Grand Central–42 St (4, 5, 6, 6X,7, 7X) 51 St (4, 6, 6X)** GRAND CENTRAL
Twenty HD TVs, roof deck with two TVs, karaoke		
234 **Paddy's** **(Patrick Maguire's)** Bar	4 p.m.–7 p.m. daily $1 off all drinks $3 PBR daily	3155 Broadway **(between La Salle & Tiemann Place) 125 St (A, B, C, D, 1)** MORNINGSIDE HEIGHTS
Pool table, jukebox		
235 **Panca** Peruvian Restaurant	4 p.m.–7 p.m. Monday–Friday $5 cocktails $5 beers $3 ceviche shots	92 Seventh Avenue South **(between Bleecker Street & Washington Place) Christopher St– Sheridan Sq (1, 2) W 4 St (A, B, C, D, E, F, M) Houston St (1, 2)** THE VILLAGE
Unique drink menu, try the tiraditos		

MONICA DiNATALE

HOURS	CONTACT	365 EXTRAS
Mon–Wed 12 p.m.–2 a.m. Thu 12 p.m.–3 a.m. Fri–Sat 12 p.m.–4 a.m. Sun 12 p.m.–12 a.m.	212-682-7266 www.overlooknyc.com	Try the pommes frites with a dozen different dipping sauces. I like the curry mayo and the red pepper aioli. Really fun atmosphere with a rooftop deck and outdoor TVs.
Daily 11 a.m.–4 a.m.	212-706-2330	They have twenty plus beers on tap and a crowd that is a mix of locals and students. Reasonable drink prices keep this place full. Feel free to order food from nearby restaurants. Toast restaurant is next door.
Mon–Thu 12 p.m.–11 p.m. Fri–Sat 12 p.m.–12 a.m.	212-488-3900 www.pancany.com	Adorable authentic Peruvian place with excellent pisco sours and floor to ceiling windows. The ceviches are amazing and all the food is fresh with interesting flavors.

WHAT	DEAL	LOCATION
236 Papatzul Mexican Restaurant	5 p.m.–8 p.m. Monday–Friday $5 sangria, bottles & drafts $6 margaritas	55 Grand Street (at West Broadway) Canal St (A, C, E,N ,R, 1, 2) SOHO
Tequila menu, live huapango or mariachi music		
237 Parea Bistro Greek Restaurant & Bar	4 p.m.–7 p.m. daily $5 beer & wine $5 appetizers like lamb tacos	36 East 20th Street (between Broadway & Park Avenue South) 23 St (4, 6, 6X, N, R) 14 St–Union Sq (N, Q, R) FLATIRON/ GRAMERCY
Excellent raw bar		
238 Parkside Lounge Bar	1 p.m.–8 p.m. daily $3 drafts, bottles & well	317 East Houston Street (at Attorney Street) Essex St (J, M, Z) Delancey St (F) 2 Av (F) LOWER EAST SIDE
Live music, comedy, pool table		

MONICA DINATALE

HOURS	CONTACT	365 EXTRAS
Mon–Wed, Sun 12 p.m.–11 p.m. Thu–Sat 12 p.m.–12 a.m.	212-274-8225 www.papatzul.com	Try the tacos taurinos. Moderately priced, each dish has an interesting aspect like a flavored sauce or salsa. The quality of the food, and the service, is excellent. Don't miss this hidden gem.
Mon–Thu, Sun 12 p.m.–10:30 p.m. Fri–Sat 12 p.m.–11:30 p.m.	212-777-8448 www.pareabistro.com	Modern swanky bistro. Lovely room with delicious fresh fish, and a $22 three-course prix-fixe dinner from 4 p.m.–7 p.m. every day. Nice for a special occasion. Steaks start at $40.
Daily 1:30 p.m.–4 a.m.	212-673-6270 www.parkside-lounge.net	They offer live entertainment every night. Check the calendar online. It's the kind of place where you'll see the latest hot band on the Lower East Side. Afforable and cool.

	WHAT	DEAL	LOCATION
239	**Pazza Notte** Italian Restaurant	5 p.m.– Close daily 2-for-1 martinis 3 p.m.–6 p.m. daily 2-for-1 wine	1375 Avenue of the Americas (between 55th & 56th Streets) 57 St–7 Av (F, N, Q, R) 7 Av (B, D, E) RADIO CITY/ ROCKEFELLER CENTER
	DJ Fridays and Saturdays		
240	**Peter McManus** Irish Pub	Daily $2 Bud & Bud Light	152 Seventh Avenue, #A (at 19th Street) 18 St (1, 2) 23 St (1, 2) 14 St (A, C, E) CHELSEA
	Jukebox		
241	**Pete's Tavern** Bar & Restaurant	Daily $5–$7 beers 5:30–7:30 Wednesday– Saturday $5 beer FREE bar snacks	129 East 18th Street (at Irving Place) 14 St–Union Sq (4, 5, 6, 6X, N, Q, R) 23 St (4, 6, 6X) UNION SQUARE
172	In 1864 O. Henry wrote "The Gift of the Magi" at Pete's Tavern.		

MONICA DiNATALE

HOURS	CONTACT	365 EXTRAS
Mon–Tue 11:30 a.m.– 10:30 p.m. Wed 11:30 a.m.– 11 p.m. Thu–Fri 11:30 a.m.– 11:30 p.m. Sat 10 a.m.– 11:30 p.m. Sun 10a.m.-10p.m.	212-765-6288 www.pazzanotepiz-za.com	Slightly north of Rock-Center, they have a large selection of martinis like lychee and mango. Modern vibe with good cracker thin crust pizza. Try the funghi portobello pizza and the prosciutto bruschetta.
Mon 11 a.m.–4 a.m. Tue–Fri 9 a.m.–4 a.m. Sat 10 a.m.–4 a.m. Sun 12 p.m.–4 a.m.	212-929-9691	Great mix of locals and whoever strolls in at this classic, vintage Irish pub. It's the kind of place that seems like it's been there forever. Good burgers, good conversation, and no fancy drinks here.
Daily 11 a.m.– 2:30 a.m.	212-473-7676 www.petestavern. com	Brick walls, dark wood and copper ceiling classic Irish Tavern. The oldest operating restaurant in New York City with tons of character. Pasta, seafood, great burgers–it has it all.

	WHAT	DEAL	LOCATION
242	**Phoenix Park** Bar & Restaurant	11:30 a.m.– 7 p.m. daily $4 drafts & well	206 East 67th Street (between 2nd & 3rd Avenues) 68 St–Hunter College (4, 6, 6X) Lexington Av/63 St (F) Lexington Av/59 St (N, Q, R) UPPER EAST SIDE
	Pool table, outdoor garden		
243	**Pig 'n' Whistle** Pub & Restaurant (3 locations)	4 p.m.–7 p.m. Monday–Friday $5 beer, wine & well	922 Third Avenue (between 55th & 56th Streets) Lexington Av/53 St (E, M) 59 St (4, 5, 6, 6X) Lexington Av/59 St (N, Q, R) MIDTOWN EAST
	Sports specials, HD TVs, live music, private rooms		
243	**Pig 'n' Whistle** Pub & Restaurant (3 locations)	4 p.m.–7 p.m. Monday–Friday $5 beer, wine & well	951 Second Avenue (between 50th & 51st Streets) 51st St (6) Lexington/53rd St (E, M) MIDTOWN EAST

Monica DiNatale

HOURS	CONTACT	365 EXTRAS
Mon–Fri 11:30 a.m.– 4 a.m. Sat–Sun 12 p.m.–4 a.m.	212-717-8181 www.phoenixparkny.com	If you lived around the corner from them, this would be the place you stop on your way from from work. Nice outdoor garden in the back and an inviting bar crowd. They carry all sports.
Daily 11 a.m.–4 a.m.	212-688-4646 www.pignwhistleon3.com	All three have a classic Irish vibe and free music on weekends. They are spacious and have high top bar tables where I like to hang. Check the website for entertainment schedules.
Daily 11 a.m.–4 a.m.	212-832-2021 www.pignwhistleon2.com	

	WHAT	DEAL	LOCATION
243	**Pig 'n' Whistle** Pub & Restaurant (3 locations)	4 p.m.–7 p.m. Monday–Friday $5 beer, wine & well	165 West 47th Street (between 6th & 7th Avenues) 47–50th (B, D, F, V) 49th (N, R, W) TIMES SQUARE/ THEATER DISTRICT/ RADIO CITY/ ROCKEFELLER CENTER
	Sports specials, HD TVs, live music, private rooms		
244	**Pine Tree Lodge** Caribbean Bar & Grill	4 p.m.–7 p.m. daily $5 2-for-1 drafts $6 2-for-1 well	591 First Avenue (at 34th Street) 33 St (4, 6, 6X) Grand Central–42 St (7, 7X) MURRAY HILL
	Live music		
245	**Planet Sushi** Japanese/Sushi Restaurant	12 p.m.–11 p.m. daily FREE saké or wine with $15 purchase per person 11 p.m.–1 a.m. daily Buy-1-get-1-FREE well	380 Amsterdam Avenue (at 78th Street) 79 St (1, 2) 72 St (1, 2, 3) 81 St–Museum of Natural History (A, B, C) UPPER WEST SIDE
	Saké menu and fresh seafood		

HOURS	CONTACT	365 EXTRAS
Mon–Fri 11:30 a.m.– 4 a.m. Sat–Sun 10:30 a.m.– 4 a.m.	212-302-0112 www.pignwhistlets.com	All three have a classic Irish vibe and free music on weekends. They are spacious and have high top bar tables where I like to hang. Check the website for entertainment schedules.
Mon–Thu 11 a.m.–2 a.m. Fri–Sat 11 a.m.–3 a.m. Sun 11 a.m.–12 a.m.	212-213-0990 www.pinetreelodge-ny.com	Jerk chicken and reasonably priced drinks are a perfect pair. Comfy, cozy rustic atmosphere with a Caribbean themed menu. Yes, they have pine covered walls and a good time vibe.
Sun–Thu 12 p.m.– 1:30 a.m. Fri–Sat 12 p.m.– 2:30 a.m.	212-712-2162 www.planetsushiny.com	The tuna tortillas are fabulous, full of fish and bursting with flavor. The menu is huge, the service is fast and the sushi is always excellent and reasonable. Fun bright décor.

	WHAT	DEAL	LOCATION
246	**Playwright Celtic Pub** Irish Pub	Until 8 p.m. daily $4 drafts $5 Cosmos	732 Eighth Avenue (between 45th & 46th Streets) 42 St–Port Authority Bus Terminal (A, C, E) 49 St (N, Q, R) 50 St (A, C, E) TIMES SQUARE/ THEATER DISTRICT
	Daily specials, private parties		
247	**Pranna** Southeast Asian Restaurant	4 p.m.–9 p.m. Monday–Friday $5 drafts $6 bottles $7 wine $8 cocktail of the day $5 wok-fired bowls	79 Madison Avenue (at 28th Street) 28 St (4, 6, 6X, N, R) 33 St (4, 6, 6X) FLATIRON/ GRAMERCY
	FREE naan with drinks, DJ		
248	**Puck Fair** Irish Pub	Daily $6 beer	298 Lafayette Street (between Jersey & East Houston Streets) Broadway–Lafayette St (B, D, F, M) Prince St (N, R) Bleecker St (4, 6, 6X) SOHO
	Sports specials		

MONICA DiNATALE

HOURS	CONTACT	365 EXTRAS
Daily 10 a.m.–4 a.m.	212-354-8404 www.playwrightcelt-icpubnyc.com	They always have reasonable drinks. $10 lunch menu Monday through Friday from 11 a.m. to 4 p.m. Right in the heart of the Theater District, they offer three floors and a rooftop garden.
Mon–Thu 4 p.m.–12 a.m. Fri 4 p.m.–4 a.m. Sat 12 p.m.–4 a.m. Sun 1 p.m.–8 p.m.	212-696-5700 www.prannarestaurant.com	Georgous bar area with huge ceilings and an Asian vibe. Later at night, the same space becomes a dance floor with club music. I go for the lychee flower martini.
Mon–Fri 11 a.m.–4 a.m. Sat–Sun 12 p.m.–4 a.m.	212-431-1200 www.puckfairbar.com	Very reasonable pub menu in a great space with a rustic feel. It's fun to sit upstairs and people watch from the open second floor. If it's crowded, try the quieter bar downstairs.

	WHAT	DEAL	LOCATION
249	**Puffy's Tavern** Bar & Italian Sandwiches	4 p.m.–8 p.m. daily $5 drafts & wine $6 well	81 Hudson Street **(at Harrison Street)** **Franklin St (1, 2)** **Chambers St (1, 2, 3)** **Canal St (A, C, E)** TRIBECA
	$4-$7 bar snacks		
250	**Punch Restaurant & Wined Up** Restaurant & Wine Bar	Punch 4 p.m.–8 p.m. daily $4 drafts $5 cocktails & wine Wined Up (Upstairs) 4 p.m.–8 p.m. daily $4 beer $5 cocktails $7 wine	913 Broadway **(between 20th & 21st Streets)** **23 St (4, 6, 6X, F, M, N, R)** FLATIRON/ GRAMERCY
	$29.95 weekend brunch includes unlimited drinks and homemade breads.		
251	**Rattle N Hum** Bar & Restaurant	11 a.m.–7 p.m. Monday–Friday $5 well, drafts & wine	14 East 33rd Street **(between 5th & Madison Avenues)** **33 St (4, 6, 6X)** **34 St–Herald Sq (B, D, F, M, N, Q, R)** **28 St (N, R)** EMPIRE STATE BUILDING
180	Four cask ales, one hundred bottles, "mug club" and "beer miles card" for prizes		

HOURS	CONTACT	365 EXTRAS
Sun–Wed 12 p.m.–1 a.m. Thu–Sat 12 p.m.–4 a.m.	212-227-3912 www. puffystavernnyc. com	Very bright window-lined corner bar. The twenty Italian artisan sandwiches and paninis are delicious on casual night out. (served until 5 p.m.) It's a low key option in the Tribeca area.
Punch Daily 11 a.m.–11 p.m. **Wined Up** Daily 5 p.m.–Close	212-673-6333 www.punchrestau-rant.com	Sleek, modern and delicious. Visit Wined Up for the true wine bar experience. Punch downstairs is slightly more formal with traditional tables for dinner. It's hard to choose just one wine!
Mon–Wed, Sun 10 a.m.–2 a.m. Thu–Sat 10 a.m.–4 a.m.	212-481-1586 www.rattlenhum-barnyc.com	If you're a beer drink-er, you'll love this place with thirty five plus beers on tap. Check online for beer tastings, rotating drafts, and brewer events. The menu includes suggested beer types for your food selection.

WHAT	DEAL	LOCATION
252 **Redemption** Bar & Restaurant	12 p.m.–7 p.m. Monday–Friday $4 beer of the day Buy-1-get-1-FREE sangria ½ price cocktails of the day ½ price appetizer of the day	1003 Second Avenue (between 53rd & 54th Streets) Lexington Av/53 St (E, M) 51 St (4, 6, 6X) 59 St (4, 5, 6, 6X) MIDTOWN EAST
Add $12 to any weekend brunch item for unlimited Bloody Marys or mimosas from 11:30 a.m.–4 p.m.		
253 **Red Egg** Chinese Restaurant & Bar	4 p.m.–7 p.m. Monday–Friday ½ price drinks 10 a.m.–12 p.m. Monday–Friday ½ price dim sum	202 Centre Street (between Grand & Hester Streets) Canal St (J, N, R, Q, Z, 4, 6, 6X) LITTLE ITALY
$7.95 lunch specials 11 a.m.–4 p.m. Monday–Friday		
254 **Reif's Tavern** Bar	4 p.m.–7 p.m. Monday–Friday $1 off bar	302 East 92nd Street (between 1st & 2nd Avenues) 86th St (4, 5, 6, 6X) 96th St (4, 6, 6X) UPPER EAST SIDE
Pool table, outdoor patio		

MONICA DiNATALE

HOURS	CONTACT	365 EXTRAS
Daily 11 a.m.–4 a.m.	212-319-4545 www.redemp-tionnyc.com	Sleek dark pub with food and drink specials that change daily. Half price appetizers like pizza, wings and calamari are a great deal. Not your typical casual pub, it's a nice spot to grab a cocktail and dinner.
Mon–Fri 11 a.m.–11 p.m. Sat–Sun 10 a.m.–11 p.m.	212-966-1123 www.redeggnyc.com	The dim sum menu is excellent and served all day. This is not your typical tiny Chinese place. It is unique to the area because it combines good food in an up-scale lounge atmosphere.
Daily 12 p.m.–4 a.m.	212-426-0519 www.reifstavern.com	You can reserve one of two grills on the back patio to grill your own food. Locals love it. Classic rock jukebox and seven TVs. You'll feel at home. Totally casual.

	WHAT	DEAL	LOCATION
255	**Riposo 46** Italian Wine Bar	4 p.m.–6 p.m. Monday–Friday 20% off wine glasses & bottles and flatbread pizzas	667 Ninth Avenue **(between 46th & 47th Streets)** **50 St (A, C, E)** **42 St–Port Authority Bus Terminal (A, C, E)** **49 St (N, Q, R)** HELL'S KITCHEN/ MIDTOWN WEST
	Flatbread pizza menu and cheese menu		
256	**Rodeo Bar** Tex/Mex Restaurant	4 p.m.–9 p.m. daily $4 drafts $6 wines $7 margaritas	375 Third Avenue **(between 27th & 28th Streets)** **23 St, 28 St, 33 St (4, 6, 6X)** FLATIRON/ GRAMERCY
	Discounted appetizer menu, FREE bar nuts, live music		
257	**Rogue** Bar & Restaurant	5 p.m.–8 p.m. Mon– Fri; Mon $4 drafts & $5 wine; Tue $4 Coors Light draft, $5 well; Wed $4 bottles & Jäger- meister shots; Thu $5 Corona & $6 margar- itas; Fri $6 martinis, $10 beer buckets; Sat–Sun $5 Bloody Mary	757 Sixth Avenue **(between 25th & 26th Streets)** **23 St (F, M)** **28 St (N, R, 1, 2)** FLATIRON/ GRAMERCY
	Sports specials, daily food specials, fourteen HD TVs		

HOURS	CONTACT	365 EXTRAS
Mon–Fri 4 p.m.–2 a.m. Sat–Sun 11:30 a.m.– 2 a.m.	212-247-8018 www.riposonyc.com	Small and charming, this is a perfect little spot to enjoy Italian wines and tempting flatbread pizzas. I especially love the wild mushroom and caramelized onion pizza. I can sit here forever.
Daily 11:30 a.m.– 4 a.m.	212-683-6500 www.rodeobar.com	Nothing but country! Check online for their schedule of FREE country, rockabilly and bluegrass live music. Enjoy the country memorabilia and a floor covered in peanut shells, while drinking your beer-ri-ta.
Mon–Wed, Sun 11 a.m.–2 a.m. Thu–Sat 11 a.m.–4 a.m.	212-242-6434 www.roguenyc.com	I consider them an upscale sports bar. Try the Irish nachos with potatoes, smoked Gouda and bacon. Twelve beers on tap. They are always looking to offer you a deal!

WHAT	DEAL	LOCATION
258 **Rudy's Bar & Grill** Bar	Daily $3 beer $7 pitchers FREE hot dogs	**627 Ninth Avenue** (between 44th & 45th Streets) 50 St (A, C, E) Times Sq–42 St (7, 7X, A, C, E) **HELL'S KITCHEN/ MIDTOWN WEST**
They brew their own beer.		
259 **Ryan's Daughter** Bar	Daily $5–$6 beers $6–$8 well	**350 East 85th Street** (between 1st & 2nd Avenues) 86 St (4, 5, 6, 6X) **UPPER EAST SIDE**
FREE chips, pool table		
260 **Ryan Maguire's Ale House** Irish Pub	Daily $3 Miller Light drafts $5 well	**28 Cliff Street** (between John & Fulton Streets) Fulton St (A, C, J, Z, 2, 3) Wall St (2, 3) **FINANCIAL DISTRICT**
FREE buffet 5 p.m.–7 p.m. Monday–Friday		

MONICA DiNATALE

HOURS	CONTACT	365 EXTRAS
Mon–Sat 8 a.m.–4 a.m. Sun 12 p.m.–4 a.m.	646-708-0890 www.rudysbarnyc.com	The FREE hot dogs alone make it worth a visit, and they are tasty! The Rudy's Blonde and Red Ales are excellent. This is a great neighborhood bar that is fun, comfortable, and reasonable.
Daily 12 p.m.–4 a.m.	212-628-2613	This laid back quintessential neighborhood bar on the Upper East Side could become habit forming. You can bring in your own food while playing pool or throwing darts.
Daily 11 a.m.–4 a.m.	212-566-6906 www.ryanmaguire-salehouse.com	Authentic Irish cuisine, mini pizzas, and great burgers. FREE drink with any brunch entrée on weekends. I like the Shepherd's Pie. They are slightly upscale and family friendly.

WHAT	DEAL	LOCATION
261 **Ryan's Irish Pub** Irish Pub	12 p.m.–8 p.m. daily, 12 a.m.–Close Sunday–Thursday $10 for 3 drafts, bottles or well	151 Second Avenue (between 9th & 10th Streets) Astor Pl (4, 6, 6X) 3 Av (L) 8 St–Nyu (N, R) EAST VILLAGE
$4 Bloody Marys and mimosas at brunch on weekends		
262 **San Marzano** Italian Restaurant	11:30 a.m.–7 p.m. daily $4 beer $ 5 wine	71 Clinton Street (between Stanton & Rivington Streets) Essex St (J, M, Z) Delancey St (F) 2 Av (F) LOWER EAST SIDE
Brick-oven pizza, weekend brunch, beer and wine only		
263 **Schiller's Liquor Bar** Restaurant & Bar	4 p.m.–7:30 p.m. Monday–Thursday, 4 p.m.–6 p.m. Friday ½ price drinks $1 oysters	131 Rivington Street (between Norfolk & Suffolk Streets) Essex St (J, M, Z) Delancey St (F) 2Av (F) LOWER EAST SIDE
Kids eat FREE 5 p.m.–7 p.m. daily.		

MONICA DiNATALE

HOURS	CONTACT	365 EXTRAS
Daily 12 p.m.–4 a.m.	212-979-9511 www.ryansnyc.com	Outdoor seating in nice weather, Ryan's has good wings and dinner specials that could include a FREE beer. Go for the trio of sliders because two just aren't enough.
Mon–Thu, Sun 11:30 a.m.– 12 a.m. Fri–Sat 11:30 a.m.– 2 a.m.	212-228-5060 www.smarzano.com	You can smell the garlic from outside. Great thin crust pizza. I like the rapini pizza with broccoli rabe and sausage. Drink up at brunch with unlimited mimosas for $18.
Mon–Thu 11 a.m.–1 a.m. Fri 11 a.m.–3 a.m. Sat 10 a.m.–3 a.m. Sun 10 a.m.–12 a.m.	212-260-4555 www.schillersny. com	If you crave dimly lit ambience and an unpretentious crowd, this place is for you. It's simply adorable with a friendly staff and comfort food. I like the pumpkin salad and the sticky toffee pudding for dessert.

	WHAT	DEAL	LOCATION
264	**Scratcher** Bar	4 p.m.–8 p.m. Monday–Saturday, 4 p.m.–7:15 p.m. Sunday $2 off drafts & well	209 East 5th Street (between Cooper Square & 2nd Avenue) Astor Pl (4, 6, 6X) 8 St–Nyu (N, R) Bleecker St (4, 6, 6X) EAST VILLAGE
	Live music, no food		
265	**Shade** Bar	12 p.m.–7 p.m. Monday–Friday $1 off beer & wine $5 well	241 Sullivan Street (between Bleecker & 3rd Streets) W 4 St (A, B, C, D, E, F, M) Christopher St–Sheridan Sq (1, 2) Houston St (1, 2) THE VILLAGE
	Grab a crêpe from the to go window. (cash only)		
266	**Shanghai Cuisine** Chinese Restaurant	Daily $6.50 martinis	89 Bayard Street (at Mulberry Street) Canal St (J, N, Q, Z, 4, 6, 6X) Chambers St (J, Z) CHINATOWN
	Martini menu, delicious soup dumplings		

MONICA DiNATALE

HOURS	CONTACT	365 EXTRAS
Daily 4 p.m.–4 a.m.	212-477-0030	A small hidden gem in this area. The kind of bar where you will find a Hollywood star and a college kid. It's comfortable and un-assuming with bench seating and corners where you can hide.
Mon–Sat 12 p.m.–4 a.m. Sun 3 p.m.–4 a.m.	212-982-6275	They serve both sweet and savory crêpes and have a reasonably priced wine list. It's a great place to grab a mar-tini and a night cap. I am a sucker for the banana Nutella crêpe.
Mon, Wed–Sun 11:30 a.m.– 10 p.m.	212-732-8988	The entire menu is a great deal at this Chinatown gem. The soup dumplings alone are worth the visit, but there is a nice drink list, reasonably priced, to enjoy with your meal. I always get a lychee martini.

	WHAT	DEAL	LOCATION
267	**Shrine** Bar & Restaurant/ Music Venue	4 p.m.–8 p.m. Monday– Saturday $3 beer $5 wine & specialty drinks $6 well $8 chicken wings & fries	2271 Adam Clayton Powell Jr. Boulevard (between 133rd & 134th Streets) 135 St (A, B, C, 2, 3) 125 St (2, 3) HARLEM
	Live music every day		
268	**Sláinte** Irish Pub	11 a.m.–7 p.m. Monday–Friday Buy-1-get-1- FREE beer, wine & well	304 Bowery (between Bleecker & Houston Streets) Bleecker St (4, 6, 6X) 2 Av (F) Broadway–Lafayette St (B, D, F, M) NOHO
	Twenty draft beers, sports specials		
269	**Slane Public House** Irish Pub	Daily $3–$4 beers $5 wine & well	102 MacDougal Street (at Bleecker Street) W 4 St (A, B, C, D, E, F, M) Houston St (1, 2) Spring St (A, C, E) THE VILLAGE
	Sporting events, DJs, live music Sundays–Thursdays		

MONICA DiNATALE

HOURS	CONTACT	365 EXTRAS
Daily 4 p.m.–4 a.m.	212-690-7807 www.shrinenyc.com	Great venue for live music with tons of character. Check the schedule online for daily music, some is FREE or have afford-able covers. You are sure to find some-thing you like. Casual menu of salads and sandwiches.
Daily 12 p.m.–4 a.m.	212-253-7030 www.slaintenyc.com	Nice pub with ex-posed brick walls, projection screen for sporting events, and an Irish affordable menu. The funnel cake fries are deli-ciously sinful.
Daily 11:30 a.m.– 4 a.m.	212-505-0079 www.slanenyc.com	They carry every rugby game. Make a reservation to re-serve your table. Be warned, they attract passionate sports fans that make for rowdy and fun crowds. No cover for live music.

	WHAT	DEAL	LOCATION
270	**Slate** Restaurant, Bar & Billiards	5 p.m.–8 p.m. Monday–Friday $4 drafts & well $5 wine $6 martinis	54 West 21st Street (between 5th & 6th Avenues) 23 St (F, M, N, R) 14 St (F, M) FLATIRON/ GRAMERCY
	Pool tables, ping-pong, private parties and rooms		
271	**Slattery's** Pub & Restaurant	3 p.m.–7 p.m. Monday–Friday, 11 a.m.–7 p.m. Saturday– Sunday $4–$6 drafts $6 martinis FREE shot with first drink	8 East 36th Street (between 5th & Madison Avenues) 33 St (4, 6, 6X) 34 St–Herald Sq (B, D, F, M, N, Q, R) Grand Central–42 St (S) MURRAY HILL
	Live music and DJs		
272	**Smith's** Bar & Restaurant	12 p.m.–7 p.m. daily $4–$5 beers $4 well & Southern Comfort shots Weekly specials	701 Eighth Avenue (between 44th & 45th Streets) 42 St–Times Sq (7, 7X, S, A, C, E) TIMES SQUARE/ THEATER DISTRICT
	Live music, sports specials		

HOURS	CONTACT	365 EXTRAS
Mon–Wed 12 p.m.–1 a.m. Thu 12 p.m.–3 a.m. Fri–Sat 12 p.m.–4 a.m. Sun 12 p.m.–12 a.m.	212-989-0096 www.slate-ny.com	Swanky sleek bar and dining area with lots of pool tables and lounge seating as well. They combine club and pool hall. An original place to throw a party or meet friends.
Mon–Sat 11 a.m.–4 a.m. Sun 12 p.m.–12 a.m.	212-683-6444 www.slatterysmid-townpub.com	All day Irish breakfast and a reasonable Irish menu with twelve beers on tap and two bars. The Midtown combo appetizer is perfect for sharing. FREE live music Wednesdays and DJ on Saturdays.
Daily 8 a.m.–4 a.m.	212-246-3268 www.smithsbar.com	In the heart of the Theater District near Times Square, Smith's has FREE live music on Wednesdays. It is a comfortable pub that is family friendly and would be a nice meeting spot if you're planning an evening in this area.

WHAT	DEAL	LOCATION
273 **Smorgas Chef** Scandinavian Restaurant & Bar (2 locations)	4 p.m.–7 p.m. daily 2-for-1 drinks	283 West 12th Street (between 4th & 8th Streets) 8 Av (L) 14 St (A, C, E, 1, 2, 3) THE VILLAGE

Local, grass-fed and organic cuisine

WHAT	DEAL	LOCATION
273 **Smorgas Chef** Scandinavian Restaurant & Bar (2 locations)	4 p.m.–7 p.m. daily 2-for-1 drinks	53 Stone Street (between Broad Street & Hanover Square) Broad St (J, Z) Wall St (2, 3) Whitehall St (N, R) FINANCIAL DISTRICT

WHAT	DEAL	LOCATION
274 **Snafu Bar** Bar	Daily $5 shots $7 margaritas, mojitos & sangria Until 8 p.m. daily $3 Bud Light pints	127 East 47th Street (between 3rd & Lexington Avenues) 51 St (4, 6, 6X) Grand Central–42 St (4, 5, 6, 6X, 7, 7X) GRAND CENTRAL/ MIDTOWN EAST

FREE popcorn, steps from Grand Central Station

MONICA DiNATALE

HOURS	CONTACT	365 EXTRAS
Mon–Fri 11 a.m.– 11:30 p.m. Sat 10:30 a.m.– 11:30 p.m. Sun 10:30 a.m.– 10:30 p.m.	212-243-7073 www.smorgas.com	Both places have a lovely upscale bistro feel. The Swedish meatballs are delicious and the meats are grass fed from their Blenheim Hill Farm. You can sit next to a tree while inside. Romantic for a date night.
Mon–Fri 11 a.m.– 10:30 p.m. Sat–Sun 10:30 a.m.– 11:30 p.m.	212-422-3500 www.smorgas.com	
Daily 11 a.m.–4 a.m.	212-317-9100 www.snafubarnyc.com	They get a nice crowd that is a cross between Midtown power players and commuters. It's divey yet comfortable with long murals and brick walls. Good pear martinis. No food.

	WHAT	DEAL	LOCATION
275	**Souths** Bar & Restaurant	4 p.m.–7 p.m. Monday–Friday $1 off bar	273 Church Street (between White & Franklin Streets) Franklin St (1, 2) Canal St (A, C, E, N, R) TRIBECA

$13 weekend brunch includes one FREE drink.

	WHAT	DEAL	LOCATION
276	**Spain** Spanish Restaurant	Daily Buy drinks & get FREE appetizers	113 West 13th Street (between 6th & 7th Avenues) 6 Av (L) 14 St (F, M, 1, 2, 3) UNION SQUARE

FREE bar snacks include meatballs and sliced potatoes.

	WHAT	DEAL	LOCATION
277	**Spin** Sports Bar, Restaurant & Ping-Pong Club	5 p.m.–7 p.m. Monday–Friday 2-for-1 well	48 East 23rd Street (between Park & Madison Avenues) 23 St (4, 6, 6X, N, R) 28 St (4, 6, 6X) FLATIRON/ GRAMERCY

Arrive before 6 p.m. for $20 per hour tables.

HOURS	CONTACT	365 EXTRAS
Daily 12 p.m.–4 a.m.	212-219-0640 www.southsnyc.com	The menu is combination Irish pub, Mexican cantina and burger joint. I like the nachos and the roasted beet salad. The large arched windows make it bright and lively for a casual date.
Daily 12 p.m.–1 a.m.	212-929-9580	Retro New York Spanish bar with the waiters to prove it! Think 1970 steakhouse. Order sangria at the bar and enjoy FREE and tasty appetizers. Remember to bring cash.
Mon 11 a.m.–12 a.m. Tue–Thu 11 a.m.–2 a.m. Fri–Sat 11 a.m.–4 a.m. Sun 11 a.m.–10 p.m.	212–982–8802 www.spingalactic.com	Two words: ping-pong. Definitely the swankiest ping-pong club around. Tons of tables and tournaments, Spin is a unique place to try on a night out with friends.

	WHAT	DEAL	LOCATION
278	**Spunto** Italian Restaurant	3:30 p.m.–6:30 p.m. daily, 3:30 p.m.–Close Monday Buy-1-get-1-FREE beer & wine FREE large pie with pitcher or bottle purchase	65 Carmine Street (between Bedford & Bleecker Streets) Houston St (1, 2) Spring St (A, C, E) Christopher St–Sheridan Sq (1, 2) THE VILLAGE
	\$5 lunch special until 5 p.m. daily includes two slices and soda.		
279	**Stand** Bar & Burgers	4 p.m.–7 p.m. Monday–Friday \$4 drafts & bottles	24 East 12th Street (between University Place & 5th Avenue) 14 St–Union Sq (4, 5, 6, 6X, L, N, Q, R) UNION SQUARE
	Amazing burgers, unique milkshake menu		
280	**Standings** Sports Bar	5 p.m.–7 p.m. Monday–Friday \$1 off drafts	43 East 7th Street (between 2nd & 3rd Avenues) Astor Pl (4, 6, 6X) 8 St–Nyu (N, R) 2 Av (F) EAST VILLAGE
208	FREE pizza 8 p.m. Fridays, FREE bagels Sundays September–January		

HOURS	CONTACT	365 EXTRAS
Mon–Thu 1 p.m.–1 a.m. Fri 11 a.m.–12 a.m. Sat 12 p.m.–12 a.m. Sun 12 p.m.–11 p.m.	212-242-1200 www.spuntothin-crust.com	Definitely check out this open air pizzeria that serves cracker thin crust pizza with delicious toppings. The classica is amazing but they have creative toppings like curried chicken and homemade chorizo worth tasting.
Mon–Thu 11 a.m.–11 p.m. Fri 11 a.m.–12 a.m. Sat 10 a.m.–12 a.m. Sun 10 a.m.–11 p.m.	212-488-5900 www.standburger.com	The burgers are memorable and so are the shakes. Nutella, toasted marshmallow and chocolate peanut butter cup are my favorites. A modern burger joint just off Union Square.
Mon–Fri 5 p.m.–2 a.m. Sat 12 p.m.–2 a.m. Sun 12 p.m.–12 a.m.	212-420-0671 www.standingsbar.com	It's a small sports bar that attracts real sports fan. Get there early if you want a seat or stand and cheer with a local crowd. Sports fans will love all the memorabilia. FREE food during football season.

WHAT	DEAL	LOCATION
281 **Stand-Up NY** Comedy Club	5 p.m.–7 p.m. daily $5–$6 well	236 West 78th Street (between Amsterdam Avenue & Broadway) 79 St (1, 2) 72 St (1, 2, 3) 81 St - Museum Of Natural History (A, B, C) UPPER WEST SIDE
Most shows are $20 with a two drink minimum.		
282 **Stillwater** Bar & Grill	11 a.m.–7 p.m. Monday–Friday $3 pints	78–80 East 4th Street (between 2nd Avenue & Bowery Street) 2 Av (F) Bleecker St (4, 6, 6X) Astor Pl (4, 6, 6X) EAST VILLAGE
Pool table, darts		
283 **Stitch** Bar & Restaurant	Until 7 p.m. daily $1 off all drinks $5 rotating drafts & sangria $7 martinis	247 West 37th Street (between 7th & 8th Avenues) 34 St–Penn Station (A, C, E) Times Sq–42 St (1, 2, 3, N, Q, R, 7, 7X) MADISON SQUARE GARDEN/ PENN STATION
Live music, DJs, party rooms		

MONICA DiNATALE

HOURS	CONTACT	365 EXTRAS
Mon–Thu 5 p.m.–12 a.m. Fri 5 p.m.–2 a.m. Sat 4 p.m.– 2 a.m. Sun 7 p.m.–12 a.m.	212-595-0850 www.standupny.com	You never know when you'll see the next big star at this classic comedy club. Jerry Seinfeld or Chris Rock may walk right through the door. It's a great place to see a show and laugh the night away.
Daily 11 a.m.–4 a.m.	212-253-2237 www.stillwaternyc.com	A neighborhood sports bar with good wings and affordable beers daily, around $5. Stop in for any sporting event, play video games and enjoy a mindless afternoon. Lunch from 11 a.m.–4 p.m. includes a FREE beer.
Mon–Fri 11 a.m.–2 a.m. Sat 5 p.m.–4 a.m.	212-852-4826 www.stitchnyc.com	The sirloin burger is choice and weighing in at twelve ounces, it's a mouthful. The large bar makes it a perfect place to meet friends after work or en route to the Theater District.

WHAT	DEAL	LOCATION
284 **Sueños** Mexican Restaurant	5 p.m.–7 p.m. Tuesday–Sunday Buy-1-get-1-FREE margaritas, sangria & beer FREE chips & salsa	311 W 17th Street (between 8th & 9th Avenues) 14 St (A, C, E) 8 Av (L) 18 St (1, 2) CHELSEA
$30 prix-fixe menu 5 p.m.–7 p.m. daily		
285 **Sushi Damo** Japanese/Sushi Restaurant	5 p.m.–7 p.m. Monday–Friday $4 drafts $5–7 wine & cocktails	330 West 58th Street (between 8th & 9th Avenues) 59 St–Columbus Circle (1, 2, A, B, C, D) 57 St–7 Av (N, Q, R) 7 Av (B, D, E) COLUMBUS CIRCLE
Try sitting at the sushi bar.		
286 **Suspenders** Bar & Restaurant	4 p.m.–Close Monday–Friday, Saturday & Sunday all day $4 drafts $5 well $10 beer & entrée 4 p.m.–6 p.m. Monday–Friday Buy-1-get-1 for ladies	111 Broadway (between Pine Street & Thames Street) Wall St (4, 5) Rector St (N, R) Broad St (J, Z) FINANCIAL DISTRICT
Trivia nights, lunch bar specials 11 a.m.–3 p.m. Monday–Friday		

204

HOURS	CONTACT	365 EXTRAS
Tue–Thu 5 p.m.–11 p.m. Fri–Sat 5 p.m.–12 a.m. Sun 5 p.m.–10 p.m.	212-243-1333 www.suenosnyc. com	Labeling itself "progressive Mexican cuisine" is bold, but true! Sueños has a delicious menu and one of the few places I found that serves micheladas and a house made sangrita with your tequila–a true Mexican treat.
Mon–Wed 12 p.m.–11 p.m. Thu–Sat 12 p.m.–12 a.m. Sun 12 p.m.– 10:30 p.m.	212-707-8609 www.sushidamo. com	In a city full of great sushi, this ranks as one of the best. The drinks will lure you here for happy hour, but the sushi will bring you back again and again. The neo and passion rolls are my favorite.
Daily 11 a.m.–2 a.m.	212-732-5005 www.suspenders- bar.com	Just north of Wall Street, Suspenders feels like a combination of a pub and a steakhouse. They offer several rotating drink and dinner specials. The burgers are enormous. Large crowds after the market closes.

WHAT	DEAL	LOCATION
287 **Sweet Revenge** Bar/Restaurant & Desserts	4 p.m.–8 p.m. Monday–Friday $5 beer $10 wine & cupcake	62 Carmine Street (at Bedford Street) Houston St (1, 2) Spring St (A, C, E) W 4 St (A, B, C, D, E, F, M) THE VILLAGE
Original concept of wine pairings with dessert		
288 **Swift Hibernian Lounge** Pub & Restaurant	Daily $6–$9 craft beers	34 East 4th Street (between Bowery & Lafayette Streets) Bleecker St (4, 6, 6X) Astor Pl (4, 6, 6X) 8 St–Nyu (N, R) NOHO
Nineteen rotating taps		
289 **Swig Bar & Grill** Bar & Grill	2 p.m.–8 p.m. Monday–Friday $4 domestic drafts $5 well Sunday–Monday $12 burger & beer	1629 Second Avenue (at 85th Street) 86th St (4, 5, 6, 6X) 77th St (4,6,6X) UPPER EAST SIDE
Outdoor seating, Tuesday trivia, soccer bar		

MONICA DiNATALE

HOURS	CONTACT	365 EXTRAS
Mon–Thu 8 a.m.–11 p.m. Fri 8 a.m.–12:30 a.m. Sat 11 a.m.–12:30 a.m. Sun 11 a.m.–9 p.m.	212-242-2240 www.sweetreveng-enyc.com	Only in New York City can you find a bakery with delicious, unique cupcakes, paired with wine. Yes, wine! On Carmine Street, sit in the window and enjoy this unique take on the Manhattan cupcake scene!
Daily 12 p.m.–4 a.m.	212-260-3600 www.swiftnycbar.com	Channel your inner beer monk in this pub with fifty four bottles and twenty three drafts. The pub menu includes cheeses, sandwiches, pizza, and shepherd's pie available until 4 a.m.
Mon–Fri 2 p.m.–4 a.m. Sat–Sun 12 p.m.–4 a.m.	212-628-2364 www.swignyc.com	Swig has a large bar menu, but also serves wraps and Irish favorites. It's a casual place to watch a game and offers sidewalk seating when warm. I love when all the windows are opened.

WHAT	DEAL	LOCATION
290 **Tap-A-Keg** Bar	Until 7 p.m. daily $1 off bar	2731 Broadway (between 104th & 105th Streets) Cathedral Pkwy (1) 103 St (A, B, C, 1) UPPER WEST SIDE
Dog friendly, pool table		
291 **Ten Degrees Bar** Bar & Restaurant	12 p.m.–8 p.m. daily 2-for-1 per person	121 St. Marks Place (between 1st Avenue & Avenue A) 1 Av (L) 2 Av (F) 3 Av (L) EAST VILLAGE
½ price wine bottles on Mondays		
292 **Terroir** Wine Bar (2 locations)	5 p.m.–7 p.m. daily $7 Wine	24 Harrison Street (between Greenwich & Hudson Streets) Franklin St (1) Chambers St (1, 2, 3) TRIBECA
They offer an enormous European wine menu so ask for help!		

MONICA DiNATALE

HOURS	CONTACT	365 EXTRAS
Mon–Fri 2 p.m.–4 a.m. Sat– Sun 12 p.m.–4 a.m.	212-749-1734	Tap-A-Keg is a dive bar with character, FREE popcorn, and reasonable drinks to accommodate the Columbia crowd nearby. The bartenders are so friendly you won't want to leave.
Daily 12 p.m.–4 a.m.	212-358-8600 www.10degreesbar.com	Unique for their olive, chocolates, meat, and cheese menus, this is a great place to nosh and have a drink. I like to chill in the front window with some friends at this contemporary wine bar. Perfect.
Mon–Sat 4 p.m.–1 a.m. Sun 4 p.m.–11 p.m.	212-625-WINE (9463) www.wineisterroir.com	These are lovely petite wine bars with eclectic small plate menus. The $7 wine deal is a find considering the quality of the wines. They often have wine events where you can try a new grape.

WHAT	DEAL	LOCATION
292 **Terroir** Wine Bar (2 locations)	5 p.m.–7p.m. daily $7 wine	439 Third Avenue (between 30th & 31st Streets) 28th & 33rd (6) MURRAY HILL

They offer an enormous European wine menu so ask for help!

293 **The 13th Step** Bar & Grill	11:30 a.m.– 8 p.m. Monday–Friday ½ price bar	149 Second Avenue (between 9th & 10th Streets) Astor Pl (4, 6, 6X) 3 Av (L) 8 St–Nyu (N, R) EAST VILLAGE

Daily rotating drink specials

294 **The Australian NYC** Australian Bar & Restaurant	4 p.m.–7 p.m. Monday–Friday $4 drafts $5 wine $6 signature cocktails $5 appetizer specials	20 West 38th Street (between 5th & 6th Avenues) 42 St–Bryant Pk (B, D, F, M) 5 Av (7, 7X) 34 St–Herald Sq (B, D, F, M, N, Q, R) EMPIRE STATE BUILDING

Twenty TVs, soccer obsessed

HOURS	CONTACT	365 EXTRAS
Mon–Thu 5 p.m.–1 a.m. Fri–Sat 5 p.m.–2 a.m. Sun 5 p.m.–11 p.m.	212-481-1920 www.wineisterroir. com	These are lovely petite wine bars with eclectic small plate menus. The $7 wine deal is a find considering the quality of the wines. They often have wine events where you can try a new grape.
Daily 11:30 a.m.– 4 a.m.	212-228-8020 www.nycbestbar. com/13thstep/	A quintessential sports bar with thirty two HD screens, a thirty four foot bar, and solid food and drink specials. Try the colossal nachos or the pulled-pork stuffed burger. Organize your group now!
Mon–Wed, Sun 11:30 a.m.– 12 a.m. Thu 11:30 a.m.– 2 a.m. Fri–Sat 11:30 a.m.– 4 a.m.	212-869-8601 www.theaustrali- annyc.com	A bit of Down Under in Midtown, with an eclectic menu of Aussie classics such as coriander crusted kangaroo, meat pies, and lamb roast to have with a cold Cooper's. Looks like an Irish pub but feels like an Aussie hangout.

	WHAT	DEAL	LOCATION
295	**The Beekman** Irish Pub	5 p.m.–7 p.m. Monday–Friday $3 Bud Light pints $5 wine & well	15 Beekman Street (at Nassau Street) Fulton St (A, C, J, Z, 2, 3) City Hall (N, R) FINANCIAL DISTRICT
	Private parties, ten TVs, sports specials		
296	**The Belgian Room & The Hop Devil Grill** Belgian Restaurant & Bar	4 p.m.–8 p.m. daily ½ price drafts, well & wine	125 St. Mark's Place (between 1st Avenue & Avenue A) 1 Av (L) 2 Av (F) 3 Av (L) EAST VILLAGE
	FREE pommes frites Mondays and Thursdays after 7 p.m.		
297	**The Central Bar** Bar & Restaurant	Until 9 p.m. daily $10–$15 pitchers $20 beer buckets (6) 3 p.m.–7 p.m. Mon–Fri $4 drafts, well, $5 wine 7 p.m.–Close Sun 2-for-1 burgers	109 East 9th Street (between Lafayette Court & Wanamaker Place) Astor Pl (4, 6, 6X) 8 St–Nyu (N, R) 3 Av (L) EAST VILLAGE
	Sports specials, dinner specials, DJs		

MONICA DiNATALE

HOURS	CONTACT	365 EXTRAS
Mon–Sat 11 a.m.–1 a.m.	212-732-7333 www.thebeekman-pub.com	Check the website for daily drink and food specials. The Beekman is one of the few downtown places serving a "perfect pint of Guinness." The Irish staff is genuinely charming.
Mon–Fri 3:30 p.m.–4 a.m. Sat–Sun 4 p.m.–4 a.m.	212-533-4467 www.belgianroomnyc.com	Two bars, sixty plus bottled craft beers and twenty five on tap. They're known for the pommes frites with several creative dipping sauces. I like the chipotle mayo.
Mon–Fri 11 a.m.–4 a.m. Sat–Sun 10 a.m.–4 a.m.	212-529-5333 www.centralbarnyc.com	Large, inviting space, that draws larger crowds on weekend nights and for big games. Downstairs has more of a pub feel. The lounge upstairs gets rowdy complete with a dance floor.

	WHAT	DEAL	LOCATION
298	**The Coliseum** Irish Pub	4 p.m.–8 p.m. Monday–Friday $5 beers & shots $6 cocktails	312 West 58th Street (between 8th & 9th Avenues) 59 St–Columbus Circle (1, 2, A, B, C, D) 57 St–7 Av (N, Q, R) 7 Av (B, D, E) COLUMBUS CIRCLE
	Sports and food specials		
299	**The Cupping Room Café** Bar & Grill	5 p.m.–8 p.m. Monday–Friday $5 drafts, wine & well	359 West Broadway (between Broome & Grand Streets) Canal St (A, C, E, 1, 2) Spring St (A, C, E) SOHO
	FREE bar food, homemade breads		
300	**The Dead Poet** Pub & Restaurant	Mon: $5 PBR & a shot 8 p.m.–Close; Tue: $5 you call it 8 p.m.– Close; Wed: $4 canned beer; Thu: $4 beer; Fri: $4 pints; Sat: $5 Bloody Mary & mimosa pints until 8 p.m., $4 canned beer 8 p.m.–Close; Sun: $5 Bloody Mary & mimosa pints	450 Amsterdam Avenue (between 81st & 82nd Streets) 79 St (1, 2) 86 St (1, 2) 81 St–Museum of Natu- ral History (A, B, C) UPPER WEST SIDE
	Nothing but deals!		

MONICA DiNATALE

HOURS	CONTACT	365 EXTRAS
Mon–Sat 11 a.m.–4 a.m. Sun 12 p.m.–4 a.m.	212-977-3523 www.thecoliseum-pub.com	Walk down the steps from 58th Street just west of Columbus Circle into this casual Irish pub with specials everyday and reasonable prices. Stop here after shopping at the nearby Time Warner Center.
Mon–Thu, Sun 8 a.m.–12 a.m. Fri–Sat 8 a.m.–2 a.m.	212-925-2898 www.cuppingroom-cafe.com	The main room is a cross between a Vermont farmhouse and a European café. This is a nice place for a date or intimate dinner serving homemade pastas and small plates. Live music Wednesday through Saturday.
Mon–Sat 10 a.m.–4 a.m. Sun 12 p.m.–4 a.m.	212-595-5670 www.thedeadpot.com	Go for the "one hundred pint club" and get your name engraved on a Guinness plaque. I'm on my way! Great cozy pub with large burgers and beers from all over the world.

	WHAT	DEAL	LOCATION
301	**The Dove Parlour** Tea Party Fare & Sandwiches	4 p.m.–8 p.m. Sunday–Thursday $7 specialty martinis, Cosmos & margaritas	228 Thompson Street (between Bleecker & West 3rd Streets) W 4 St (A, B, C, D, E, F, M) Broadway–Lafayette St (B, D, F, M) Bleecker St (4, 6, 6X) THE VILLAGE
	Cheese menu and tea sandwiches		
302	**The Dubliner** Irish Pub	Daily $5 beer 9 p.m.–1 a.m. Monday–Wednesday $.25 wings	45 Stone Street (between Coenties Alley & Mill Lane) Broad St (J, Z) Whitehall St (N, R) Wall St (2, 3) FINANCIAL DISTRICT
	Weekend brunch includes one FREE beverage.		
303	**The East End Tavern** Bar	Until 7 p.m. daily $4 pints & well	1589 First Avenue (between 82nd & 83rd Streets) 86 St (4, 5, 6, 6X) 77 St (4, 6, 6X) UPPER EAST SIDE
216	Eight HD TVs, sports specials		

HOURS	CONTACT	365 EXTRAS
Daily 4 p.m.–4 a.m.	212-254-1435 www.thedoveparlour.com	Designed to look like the parlour room of an old New York City brownstone, you'll find lovely "tea party" fare, boutique wines, inventive cocktails and a friendly staff. Try the red velvet sparkler.
Daily 11 a.m.–3 a.m.	212-785-5400 www.dublinernyc.com	Set on cobblestoned, Stone Street in the Wall Street area, you'll feel like you're stepping into Ireland. Outdoor seating when warm that is great for people watching. Daily rotating drink specials
Daily 12 p.m.–4 a.m.	212-249-5960 www.eastend-tavernnyc.com	Serious "drinking consultants" reside at this Upper East Side neighborhood sports bar with great specials daily. You can order food from nearby restaurants when hungry.

	WHAT	DEAL	LOCATION
304	**The Empire Hotel Rooftop** Lounge	5 p.m.–8 p.m. Monday–Friday $5–$6 beer $8 wine & well	44 West 63rd Street (12th floor, between Columbus Avenue & Broadway) 66 St–Lincoln Center (1, 2) 59 St–Columbus Circle (1, 2, A, B, C, D) 72 St (A, B, C) LINCOLN CENTER
	DJs Wednesdays–Saturdays		
305	**The Four–Faced Liar** Bar	Daily $6 PBR & shot 2 p.m.–8 p.m. daily $1 off everything	165 West 4th Street (between Jones & Cornelia Streets) W 4 St (A, B, C, D, E, F, M) Christopher St–Sheridan Sq (1, 2) Houston St (1, 2) THE VILLAGE
	Live music, ten beers on tap		
306	**The Gael Pub** Irish Pub	Until 8 p.m. Monday–Friday $4 drafts $5 well & wine	1465 Third Avenue (between 82nd & 83rd Streets) 86 St (4, 5, 6, 6X) 77 St (4, 6, 6X) UPPER EAST SIDE
218	Rotating specials, trivia, guest bartending, DJs, pool table		

MONICA DiNATALE

HOURS	CONTACT	365 EXTRAS
Sun–Wed 5 p.m.–12 a.m. Thu–Sat 5 p.m.–4 a.m.	212-956-3313 www.chinagrillmgt.com	This is a large rooftop lounge with two outdoor patios and great views of Lincoln Center and the entire Upper West Side. It's a sexy space with beautiful ambiance at sunset.
Daily 2 p.m.–4 a.m.	212-206-8959 www.the-four-facedliar.com	Comfortable neighborhood bar with live music on Wednesdays. This is the kind of place locals love. Nothing but reasonable drinks and good Irish conversation. Order in food from nearby restaurants.
Mon–Fri 5 p.m.–4 a.m. Sat–Sun 12 p.m.–4 a.m.	212-517-4141 www.thegael-pubnyc.com	There is a different drink special every night after 8 p.m., and Tuesday is trivia night. Relaxed Irish pub with live music, guest bartending and sporting events. I prefer sitting near the projector screen in the back.

	WHAT	DEAL	LOCATION
307	**The Gin Mill** Bar & Grill	11:30 a.m.– 8 p.m. daily ½ price drinks	442 Amsterdam Avenue **(between 81st & 82nd Streets)** **79 St (1, 2)** **86 St (1, 2)** **81 St–Museum of Natural History (A, B, C)** UPPER WEST SIDE
	Daily drink specials, sports specials		
308	**The Ginger Man** Bar & Restaurant	Daily $6.50 beers	11 East 36th Street **(between 5th & Madison Avenues)** **33 St (4, 6, 6X)** **34 St–Herald Sq (B, D, F, M, N, Q, R)** **Grand Central–42 St (S)** EMPIRE STATE BUILDING
	Three hundred beers, growlers to go and special beer events on website		
309	**The Globe** Bar & Restaurant	11:30 a.m.– 7 p.m. daily $5 drafts, bottles & well $7 wine	158 East 23rd Street **(between 3rd & Lexington Avenues)** **23 St (4, 6, 6X, N, R)** **28 St (4, 6, 6X)** FLATIRON/ GRAMERCY
220	Fireplace		

HOURS	CONTACT	365 EXTRAS
Mon–Sat 11:30 a.m.– 4 a.m. Sun 12 p.m.–4 a.m.	212-580-9080 www.nycbestbar. com/ginmill	They always have a passionate sports crowd. In warmer months it's filled with teams from Central Park. You will consistently find good deals at this grill right in the heart of the Upper West Side.
Mon–Thu 11:30 a.m.– 2 a.m. Fri 11:30 a.m.– 4 a.m. Sat 12:30 p.m.– 4 a.m. Sun 12:30 p.m.– 2 a.m.	212-532-3740 www.gingerman-ny. com	This is a beer lover's paradise with seventy beers on tap and over one hundred by the bottle. It's always reasonable and almost overwhelming to choose your pint. Take your time and enjoy.
Daily 11:30 a.m.– 4 a.m.	212-477-6161 www.theglobeny. com	I like that they offer beef, buffalo, turkey, veggie and kobe burgers with tons of toppings. Try the hummus plate too. $10 burger and beer lunch Monday through Friday 11:30p.m.– 4 p.m.

WHAT	DEAL	LOCATION
310 **The Half King** Pub & Restaurant	5 p.m.–8 p.m. daily $4 drafts $7 drink specials	505 West 23rd Street (at 10th Avenue) 23 St (A, C, E) CHELSEA
Their Monday "reading series" hosts about fifty literary events a year.		
311 **The Half Pint** Pub & Restaurant	4 p.m.–6 p.m. Monday–Friday $5 drafts & well	76 West 3rd Street (at Thompson Street & LaGuardia Place) W 4 St (A, B, C, D, E, F, M) Broadway–Lafayette St (B, D, F, M) 8 St–Nyu (N, R) THE VILLAGE
Two hundred beers, twenty plus on tap, cask ale		
312 **The Heights** Bar & Grill	3 p.m.–7 p.m. daily, 11 p.m.–Close daily $4 drafts & wine $5 frozen margaritas	2867 Broadway (between 111th & 112th Streets) Cathedral Pkwy (1) 116 St–Columbia University (1) 103 St (1) MORNINGSIDE HEIGHTS
Outdoor rooftop patio with heaters		

HOURS	CONTACT	365 EXTRAS
Mon–Fri 11 a.m.–4 a.m. Sat–Sun 9 a.m.–4 a.m.	212-462-4300 www.thehalfking.com	The three owners are all writers, including Sebastian Junger, author of "The Perfect Storm." I've gone out of my way for the burger here. The garden seating in the back is adorable.
Mon 12 p.m.–2 a.m. Tue–Fri 12 p.m.–4 a.m. Sat 10 a.m.–4 a.m. Sun 10 a.m.–2 a.m.	212-260-1088 www.thehalfpint.com	This is a great beer bar with an outstanding fried appetizer selection. The staff is knowledgeable and the prices reasonable. Add $12 to your brunch for unlimited Bloody Marys or mimosas on weekends. Beer heaven.
Mon–Fri 11:30 a.m.–3 a.m. Sat–Sun 11 a.m.–3 a.m.	212-866-7035 www.theheightsnyc.com	I like the rooftop bar for drinks or dinner in this Columbia neighborhood. The main dining room has a jazzy relaxed feel. Try the mango margarita or the half-priced bottle of wine with entrée on Mondays.

	WHAT	DEAL	LOCATION
313	**The Hog Pit** Bar & Restaurant	Daily $3 PBRs $4 drafts $12 pitchers	37 West 26th Street (between Broadway & 6th Avenue) 28 St (N, R) 23 St (F, M, N, R) FLATIRON/ GRAMERCY
	Pool table, Big Buck Hunter, darts		
314	**The House of Brews** Bar & Restaurant (2 locations)	11 a.m.–7 p.m. Monday–Friday $1 off beers $5 margaritas & Cosmos	302 West 51st Street (between 8th & 9th Avenues) 50 St (A, C, E, 1, 2) 49 St (N, Q, R) HELL'S KITCHEN/ MIDTOWN WEST
	Sports specials, beer events		
314	**The House of Brews** Bar & Restaurant (2 locations)	11 a.m.–7 p.m. Monday–Friday $1 off beers $5 margaritas & Cosmos	363 West 46th Street (between 8th & 9th Avenues) 50 St (A, C, E) 42 St–Port Authority Bus Terminal (A, C, E) 49 St (N, Q, R) TIMES SQUARE/ THEATER DISTRICT

MONICA DiNATALE

HOURS	CONTACT	365 EXTRAS
Sun–Mon 11:30 a.m.– 2 a.m. Tue 11:30 a.m.– 3 a.m. Wed–Sat 11:30 a.m.– 4 a.m.	212-213-4871 www.hogpit.com	You will smell the barbecue down the block. Rowdy atmosphere and solid food make this place a winner with groups. Try the brisket and the pulled pork sliders. $3 beers attract sports fans as well.
Daily 11 a.m.–4 a.m.	212-541-7080 www.houseof-brewsny.com	There are sixty plus beers available from around the world for the true beer lover. It's a nice choice for a casual dinner before a show. You can always find a $6 beer and drink and food specials.
Daily 11 a.m.–4 a.m.	212-245-0551 www.houseof-brewsny.com	

	WHAT	DEAL	LOCATION
315	**The Irish Exit** Irish Pub	Tuesday 2-for-1 drinks from 8 p.m., FREE comedy; Wednesday $4 drafts, Quiz Night; Thursday $1 PBR; Thursday & Friday 2-for-1, $5 at the door 6 p.m.–9 p.m.; Saturday–Sunday sports specials like $3 drafts	978 Second Avenue (at 52nd Street) Lexington Av/53 St (E, M) 51 St (4, 6, 6X) 59 St (4, 5, 6, 6X) MIDTOWN EAST
	Brunch includes two FREE drinks. Check the website for rotating drink specials and comedy shows.		
316	**The Library** Bar	5 p.m.–8 p.m. daily Buy-1-get-1-FREE bar	7 Avenue A (between 1st & 2nd Streets) 2 Av (F) Delancey St (F) Essex St (J, M, Z) EAST VILLAGE
	Jukebox		
317	**The Long Room** Bar & Restaurant	Daily $1 oysters $6 drafts	120 West 44th Street (between Broadway & 6th Avenue) 42 St–Bryant Pk (B, D, F, M) Times Sq–42 St (1, 2, 3, N, Q, R, S) TIMES SQUARE/THEATER DISTRICT
	Breweries of the month, sports specials		

MONICA DiNATALE

HOURS	CONTACT	365 EXTRAS
Daily 11 a.m.–4 a.m.	212-755-8383 www.irishexitnyc.com	It's Pittsburgh Steelers and Iowa Hawkeye country here during football season. The Irish Exit is a good pick for sporting events and food specials. I like the slider menu and the "New Jersey" with meatballs and marinara.
Daily 12 p.m.–4 a.m.	212-375-1352	Eclectic, dive bar atmosphere. Great drink specials, B-movies and a jukebox with excellent variety. This is a drinker's haven for the local hipsters. Yes, it's filled with books and couches.
Mon 11:30 a.m.– 2 a.m. Tue–Fri 11:30 a.m.– 4 a.m. Sat 11 a.m.–4 a.m. Sun 11 a.m.–2 a.m.	212-997-3933 www.thelong-roomnyc.com	Large sophisticated bar with leather booths, a fireplace, and forty plus beers on tap. Try the Thanksgiving day dinner on ciabatta. A good place to take a break from the hustle of Times Square.

WHAT	DEAL	LOCATION
318 **The Mad Hatter** Irish Pub	11 a.m.–8 p.m. Monday–Wednesday, 11 a.m.–7 p.m. Thursday–Friday $4 drafts $5 wine & well $6 martini & Cosmos	360 Third Avenue **(between 26th & 27th Streets)** 23 St, 28 St, 33 St 4, 6, 6X FLATIRON/ GRAMERCY
Soccer bar, jukebox, pool table, karaoke		
319 **The Mean Fiddler** Bar & Restaurant	12 p.m.–8 p.m. daily $4–$6 beers $6 well & cocktails $.75 wings	266 West 47th Street **(between Broadway & 8th Avenue)** 49 St (N, Q, R) 50 St (A, C, E, 1, 2) TIMES SQUARE/ THEATER DISTRICT
Pittsburgh Steelers and Philadelphia Eagles bar, private room, karaoke, sports specials		
320 **The Mermaid Inn/Oyster Bar** Seafood Restaurant **(3 locations)**	5:30 p.m.–7:30 p.m. Monday–Thursday, 5 p.m.–7 p.m. Saturday–Sunday $1 oysters & clams $3–8 appetizers $5 drafts $6 wine	**(Mermaid Oyster Bar)** 79 MacDougal Street **(between Bleecker & West Houston Streets)** Houston St (1, 2) Spring St (A, C, E) W 4 St (A, B, C, D, E, F, M) THE VILLAGE
Try the lobster sliders!		

MONICA DiNATALE

HOURS	CONTACT	365 EXTRAS
Daily 11 a.m.–4 a.m.	212-696-2122 www.madhattersaloonnyc.com	The outdoor beer garden alone is worth a trip at this home of Manchester City Football Club. Tons of deals for drinks and food, including lunch specials. Want to sit outside, have a drink, watch a game, this is the place.
Daily 10 a.m.–4 a.m.	212-354-2950 www.themeanfiddlernyc.com	Combination of a dive bar, dance club and karaoke bar, which makes for an interesting mix of people. Unpretentious, so no need to dress up. Drink specials daily and Guinness on tap.
Mon–Thu 5:30 p.m.– 11 p.m. Fri–Sat 5 p.m.– 11:30 p.m. Sun 5 p.m.–10 p.m.	212-260-0100 www.themermaidnyc.com	Delicious seafood restaurant! The food deals will save you some serious cash. I like the fish tacos and the oysters. It's worth waiting for a seat, but get there early to improve your chances.

WHAT	DEAL	LOCATION
320 **The Mermaid Inn/Oyster Bar** Seafood Restaurant (3 locations)	5 p.m.–7 p.m. daily $1 oysters & clams $3–8 appetizers $5 drafts $6 wine	96 Second Avenue (between 5th & 6th Avenues) Astor Pl (4, 6, 6X) 2 Av (F) 8 St–Nyu (N, R) EAST VILLAGE
Try the lobster sliders!		
320 **The Mermaid Inn/Oyster Bar** Seafood Restaurant (3 locations)	5 p.m.–7 p.m. daily $1 oysters & clams $3–8 appetizers $5 drafts $6 wine	568 Amsterdam Avenue (between 87th & 88th Streets) 86 St (B, C, 1) 96 St (1, 2, 3, A, B, C, D) UPPER WEST SIDE
321 **The Parlour** Irish Pub (2 locations)	Until 7 p.m. Monday–Friday $3 domestic bottles & drafts $4 wine & well	250 West 86th Street (at Broadway) 86 St (1, 2) 79 St (1, 2) 96 St (1, 2, 3) UPPER WEST SIDE
230 Food and drink specials online		

MONICA DiNATALE

HOURS	CONTACT	365 EXTRAS
Mon 5:30 p.m.– 10 p.m. Tue–Fri 5:30 p.m.– 11 p.m. Sat 11 a.m.– 11 p.m. Sun 11 a.m.– 10 p.m.	212-674-5870 www.themermaidnyc.com	Delicious seafood restaurant! The food deals will save you some serious cash. I like the fish tacos and the oysters. It's worth waiting for a seat, but get there early to improve your chances.
Mon 5 p.m.–10 p.m. Tue–Fri 5 p.m.– 10:30 p.m. Sat 11 a.m.– 10:30 p.m. Sun 11 a.m.–10 p.m.	212-799-7400 www.themermaidnyc.com	
Daily 11 a.m.–4 a.m.	212-580-8923 www.theparlour.com	I love the atmosphere at these Irish pubs on the Upper Sides with an extensive menu and friendly bartenders right from the Emerald Isle. Sports specials, dancing, live music and karaoke on weekends.

	WHAT	**DEAL**	**LOCATION**
321	**The Parlour** Irish Pub (2 locations)	Until 7 p.m. Monday–Friday $3 domestic bottles & drafts $4 wine & well	1804 Second Avenue (between 93rd & 94th Streets) 96 St (6) UPPER EAST SIDE
	Food and drink specials online		
322	**The Patriot Saloon** Bar	Daily $3 drafts & shots $6 cocktails $6.50–$13 pitchers	110 Chambers Street (between Church Street & Broadway) Chambers St (1, 2, 3, A, C) City Hall (N, R) TRIBECA
	Cash only, jukebox		
323	**The Pizza Pub** Bar	Daily FREE slice with shot purchase 1 p.m.–7 p.m. daily $3 well & beer $5 beer & pizza $24 pie and pitcher $27 pie & wine bottle	294 Third Avenue (between 22nd & 23rd Streets) 23 St (4, 6, 6X, N, R) 28 St (4, 6, 6X) FLATIRON/ GRAMERCY
	Sports specials		

MONICA DiNATALE

HOURS	CONTACT	365 EXTRAS
Daily 11 a.m.–4 a.m.	212-722-6300 www.theparlour.com	I love the atmosphere at these Irish pubs on the Upper Sides with an extensive menu and friendly bartenders right from the Emerald Isle. Sports specials, dancing, live music and karaoke on weekends.
Daily 11:30 a.m.– 4 a.m.	212-748-1162	A true old dive bar with Johnny Cash on the jukebox, outstanding drink prices, sexy bartenders, and a serious good time vibe. They always offer cheap food specials like $3 chili dogs and beer deals.
Mon–Wed 11:30 a.m.– 1 a.m. Thu–Sat 11:30 a.m.– 4 a.m.	212-477-8100	Gotta love FREE pizza with beer. Be careful, those shots will sneak up on you. A change of pace from the Irish pub Third Avenue bar scene. It's a casual hang out bar. The pizza is delightful at the end of a long evening.

	WHAT	DEAL	LOCATION
324	**The Pony Bar** Pub & Restaurant	4:20 p.m.– 5:20 p.m. daily $4 beers $6 beers all other times	637 Tenth Avenue (at 45th Street) 42 St–Port Authority Bus Terminal (A, C, E) 50 St (A, C, E) HELL'S KITCHEN/ MIDTOWN WEST
	Check the website for tasting schedules and guest brewery tastings. **(new location on UPPER EAST SIDE)**		
325	**The Sixth Ward** Bar & Restaurant	4 p.m.–4 a.m. Monday– Wednesday, 12 p.m.–7 p.m. Thursday–Friday, 4 p.m.–11 p.m. Saturday, 4 p.m.–4 a.m. Sunday $3 shots $4 beer & well Daily drink specials	191 Orchard Street (between Stanton & Houston Streets) 2 Av (F) Delancey St (F) Essex St (J, M, Z) LOWER EAST SIDE
	Pool table, trivia, jukebox, DJs, beer garden		
326	**The Snug** Bar	3 p.m.–7 p.m. & 11 p.m.–1 a.m. Monday– Thursday $3 PBR $4 well, martinis & drafts	751 Ninth Avenue (between 50th & 51st Streets) 50 St (A, C, E, 1, 2) 49 St (N, Q, R) HELL'S KITCHEN/ MIDTOWN WEST
234	Tons of drink and sports specials		

MONICA DiNATALE

HOURS	CONTACT	365 EXTRAS
Mon–Fri 3 p.m.–4 a.m. Sat–Sun 12 p.m.–4 a.m.	212-586-2707 www.theponybar.com	Craft beer bar with a local vibe and a rotating selection of beers including at least two cask ales. I love this place and go in for one and come out three or four later. The quality of beers available for the price can't be beat.
Mon–Wed 4 p.m.–4 a.m. Thu–Fri 12 p.m.–4 a.m. Sat–Sun 11 a.m.–4 a.m.	212-228-9888 www.thesixthward.com	I like the enclosed beer garden in the back. Much cooler than the average sports bar. The weekend brunch special includes two hours of FREE mimosas and Bloody Marys for $15 from 11 a.m.–4 p.m.
Mon–Wed 2:30 p.m.–4 a.m. Thu–Sun 11 a.m.–4 a.m.	212-632-1783 www.thesnug-barnyc.com	Laid back Ninth Avenue bar where you're sure to make new friends. Cozy space hosts some locals, some tourists, some Midtown work crowd. Stop here for a late night night cap.

	WHAT	DEAL	LOCATION
327	**The Spring Lounge** Bar	5 p.m.–7 p.m. Monday–Friday $1 off drafts	48 Spring Street (at Mulberry Street) Spring St (4, 6, 6X) Bowery (J) Prince St (N, R) NOHO
	FREE bagels Sundays 12 p.m., FREE hotdogs Wednesdays 5 p.m.–7 p.m.		
328	**The Stag's Head** Bar	11 a.m.–7 p.m. Monday–Friday $4 well $4–$5 craft beer drafts	252 East 51st Street (between 2nd & 3rd Avenues) Lexington Av/53 St (E, M) 51 St (4, 6, 6X) 5 Av/53 St (E, M) MIDTOWN EAST
	Craft beers and guest breweries		
329	**The Stumble Inn** Sports Bar & Grill	11:30 a.m.– 7 p.m. Monday–Friday ½ price bar	1454 Second Avenue (between 75th & 76th Streets) 77 St (4, 6, 6X) 68 St–Hunter College (4, 6, 6X) UPPER EAST SIDE
236	FREE draft beer or soda with any stuffed burger 11:30 a.m.–4 p.m. Monday–Friday		

MONICA DiNATALE

HOURS	CONTACT	365 EXTRAS
Mon–Sat 8 a.m.–4 a.m. Sun 12 p.m.–4 a.m.	212-965-1774 www.thespringlounge.com	A gem in the area with fair prices and an unpretentious mood. Twelve beers on tap. There are bars in the neighborhood for the "scene", but come here if you want a relaxing drink with friends.
Mon–Sat 11 a.m.–4 a.m. Sun 12 p.m.–4 a.m.	212-888-2453 www.thestagsheadnyc.com	It looks like a hunting lodge but acts like a beer bar. Fifty plus beers on tap and a seasonal cocktail menu. Try the "Mr. Claus" during the holidays. The beer sampler is the way to go for beer lovers.
Daily 11:30 a.m.–4 a.m.	212-650-0561 www.nycbestbar.com/stumble/	Stuffed burgers that explode with flavor and cheese. Yum. "Stumble Inn" for sports with fourteen HD TVs and specials during the games.

|---|---|---|---|
330	**The Tangled Vine** Wine Bar & Restaurant	5 p.m.–7 p.m. Monday–Friday $1 oysters $4–$5 appetizers $4 beer $6 wine	434 Amsterdam Avenue (at 81st Street) 79 St (1, 2) 86 St (1, 2) 81 St–Museum of Natural History (A, B, C) UPPER WEST SIDE
	30% off bottles Mondays, food specials		
331	**The Ten Bells** Wine Bar	Daily $1.25 oysters $6–$12 wine	247 Broome Street (between Ludlow & Orchard Streets) Delancey St (F) Essex St (J, M, Z) Grand St (B, D) LOWER EAST SIDE
	Beer and wine only, cheese and cured meats menu		
332	**The Thirsty Scholar** Irish Pub	5 p.m.–8 p.m. daily $4 well $4–$5 drafts $5 wine $7 martinis, Manhattans & Cosmos	155 Second Avenue (at 10th Street) Astor Pl (4, 6, 6X) 3 Av (L) 8 St–Nyu (N, R) EAST VILLAGE
	Check website weekly for special events.		

MONICA DINATALE

HOURS	CONTACT	365 EXTRAS
Sun–Mon 5 p.m.–12 a.m. Tue–Thu 5 p.m.–1 a.m. Fri 5 p.m.–2 a.m. Sat 4 p.m.–2 a.m.	646-863-3896 www.tangledvine-bar.com	I like the meatballs and the grilled bread with ricotta. It's an inviting bright wine bar with a wine list that spans the globe. You may have to wait for a spot at the bar but it's worth it.
Mon–Fri 5 p.m.–2 a.m. Sat–Sun 3 p.m.–2 a.m.	212-228-4450 www.thetenbells.com	Absolutely stunning oak wood bar with high ceilings and floral arrangements make this a romantic spot. The tapas menu is perfect for sharing. There are communal tables in the back rooms. Mostly French and Italian wines.
Daily 2 p.m.–4 a.m.	212-777-6514 www.thethirsty-scholar.com	Channel your inner poet with inventive martinis or try reading the poetry on the walls for inspiration. They sometimes offer FREE bar food but they don't have a menu.

WHAT	DEAL	LOCATION
333 **The Trailer Park Lounge** Bar & Restaurant	4 p.m.–6 p.m. daily $3 drafts & cans $5 margaritas $6 off margarita pitchers	271 West 23rd Street (between 7th & 8th Avenues) 23 St (A, C, E, 1, 2) 28 St (1, 2) FLATIRON/ GRAMERCY
Lunch specials include one FREE draft beer 12 p.m.–4 p.m. daily.		
334 **The Underground** Bar/Restaurant/ Live Music & Comedy	4 p.m.–7 p.m. Monday–Friday $5 beer & margaritas $6 wine Sunday & Monday $.75 wings	955 West End Avenue (at 107th Street) Cathedral Pkwy (1) 103 St (1) 116 St–Columbia University (1) UPPER WEST SIDE
Food specials daily, live music, comedy		
335 **The Uptown Lounge Restaurant & Bar** Restaurant & Lounge	4 p.m.–8 p.m. daily $4 beers $6 martinis, wine & sangria	1576 Third Avenue (between 88th & 89th Streets) 86 St (4, 5, 6, 6X) 96 St (4, 6, 6X) UPPER EAST SIDE
50% off bottles Mondays, live music and DJs on Fridays and Saturdays		

MONICA DiNATALE

HOURS	CONTACT	365 EXTRAS
Daily 12 p.m.–3 a.m.	212-463-8000 www.trailerpark-lounge.com	Totally kitschy bar meant to transport you out of New York and into the country. Grab your cowboy hat and take advantage of affordable drinks, burgers and a good time.
Mon–Fri 4 p.m.–4 a.m. Sat–Sun 12 p.m.–4 a.m.	212-531-4759 www.theunder-groundnyc.com	Unique small place to see live music and comedy. Check the busy schedule online. Yes, it's a basement but it's cool. Impress your friends with this find.
Daily 12 p.m.–1 a.m. (4 a.m. if busy)	212-828-1388 www.theuptown-restaurantandbar.com	Great uptown destination with extensive menu of wine, beer, and martinis. Rustic wine bar, lounge type atomosphere with a touch of class. The back room is full of skylights so you'll feel like you're getting a tan!

	WHAT	DEAL	LOCATION
336	**The Village Tavern** Sports Bar	4 p.m.–7 p.m. Monday–Friday $4 well & 20 ounce pints of Yuengling, Bud Light & Rolling Rock; 12 p.m.–7 p.m. Saturday–Sunday $4 well & 20 ounce pints of Yuengling, Bud Light & Rolling Rock & $10 pitchers	46 Bedford Street (at Leroy Street) Houston St (1, 2) Christopher St–Sheridan Sq (1, 2) W 4 St (A, B, C, D, E, F, M) THE VILLAGE
	Ten HD TVs, pool table, jukebox, Golden Tee Live		
337	**The Watering Hole** Bar & Restaurant	4 p.m.–7 p.m. Monday–Friday $5 drafts, well & wine 5:30 p.m.–6:30 p.m. FREE buffet	106 East 19th Street (between Park Avenue South & Irving Place) 23 St (4, 6, 6X) 14 St–Union Sq (4, 5, 6, 6X, N, Q, R) FLATIRON/ GRAMERCY
	$12 lunch special includes a FREE beer or glass of wine.		
338	**The Whiskey Rebel** Bar	Daily $5 specialty martinis & shots Until 7 p.m. daily $3 Bud Light drafts $5 well & Cosmos	129 Lexington Avenue (between 28th & 29th Streets) 28 St (4, 6, 6X) 33 St (4, 6, 6X) 23 St (4, 6, 6X) MURRAY HILL
	Sports specials, discounts for alumni groups		

HOURS	CONTACT	365 EXTRAS
Mon–Fri 4 p.m.–4 a.m. Sat– Sun 12 p.m.–4 a.m.	212-741-1935 www.village-tavernnyc.com	Perfectly situated on the corner of Bedford Street, you will simply have to stop by for a drink. Twelve beers on tap and tons of drink specials. They carry all sports and have a pool table in the back room.
Mon–Sat 11 a.m.–4 a.m. Sun 12 p.m.–4 a.m.	212-674-5783 www.wateringho-lenyc.com	FREE karaoke makes everyone a superstar. Inexpensive, FREE food and fun. What more do you need? I like the chili and the grilled steak wrap. Steps from Gramercy Park without the high prices.
Daily 11:30 a.m.– 4 a.m.	212-686-3800 www.whiskeyre-belnyc.com	The dark wood bar and murals on the walls provide a "Pro-hibition" era feel that makes this a very inviting spot to drink whiskey or cocktails. $4 beers after 9 p.m. daily and FREE pop-corn.

	WHAT	DEAL	LOCATION
339	**The Whiskey Ward** Bar	5 p.m.–8 p.m. Monday–Saturday $4 well & drafts, $5 margaritas & $15 sangria pitchers; Sunday all night $5 margaritas & Manhattans; Sunday 6 p.m.–9 p.m. $4 well & drafts	121 Essex Street (between Rivington & Delancey Streets) Delancey St (F) Essex St (J, M, Z) 2 Av (F) LOWER EAST SIDE
	Whiskey flights and tastings, "taste of whiskey" one ounce pour		
340	**Third & Long** Sports Bar	Daily $1–$4 drink specials 5 p.m.–9 p.m. daily $5 beer	523 Third Avenue (between 34th & 35th Streets) 33 St (4, 6, 6X) Grand Central–42 St (4, 5, 6, 6X, 7, 7X) MURRAY HILL
	Trivia Wednesdays, rotating drink specials		
341	**Three of Cups** Italian Restaurant	5 p.m.–8 p.m. at bar, 8 p.m.–9 p.m. in lounge daily $4 beer, well & wine	83 First Avenue (at 5th Street) 2 Av (F) Delancey St (F) Bleecker St (4, 6, 6X) EAST VILLAGE
244	20% off bill Monday–Thursday 5 p.m.–6 p.m., comedy, live music		

HOURS	CONTACT	365 EXTRAS
Mon–Sat 5 p.m.–4 a.m. Sun 6 p.m.–4 a.m.	212-477-2998 www.thewhiskey-ward.com	They have a great selection of whiskeys. Check the website for a full list or stop in and try a whiskey flight. You can always try a one ounce pour to find your favorite.
Daily 11 a.m.–3 a.m.	212-447-5711 www.thirdandlongnyc.com	There are always amazing deals at this popular somewhat upscale sports bar. Sixteen beers on tap. A good place to catch a beer and check the score. No food.
Sun–Thu 5 p.m.–12 a.m. Fri–Sat 12 p.m.– 2 a.m.	212-388-0059 www.threeof-cupsnyc.com	Great corner location, comfortable, with cool atmosphere. I am a big fan of the wood-burning oven and dream about the artichoke pizza. The lounge downstairs plays rock n' roll seven days a week.

	WHAT	DEAL	LOCATION
342	**Three Sheets Saloon** Sports Bar	8 p.m.–Close Monday–Thursday $3 beer & shots 2 p.m.–8 p.m. Friday, 12 p.m.–8 p.m. Saturday ½ price bar 12 p.m.–Close Sunday ½ price beer	134 West 3rd Street (between 6th Avenue & MacDougal Street) W 4 St (A, B, C, D, E, F, M) Christopher St–Sheridan Sq (1, 2) Houston St (1, 2) THE VILLAGE
	Tons of rotating specials, twenty four HD TVs, beer pong		
343	**Thunder Jackson's** Bar & Restaurant	11:30 a.m.– 7 p.m. Monday–Friday $3 beer, sangria & well $8 burger & beer	169 Bleecker Street (between Bleecker & West 3rd Streets) W 4 St (A, B, C, D, E, F, M) Spring St (A, C, E) Houston St (1, 2) THE VILLAGE
	Jukebox, sports specials		
344	**Toast** Restaurant & Bar (2 locations)	5 p.m.–8 p.m. daily $1 off drinks	2737 Broadway (at 105th Street) 103 St (A, B, C, 1) UPPER WEST SIDE
246	House-cured salmon and pork, sixteen beers on tap, $7 beer flights		

MONICA DiNATALE

HOURS	CONTACT	365 EXTRAS
Mon–Fri 2 p.m.–4 a.m. Sat–Sun 12 p.m.–4 a.m.	212-777-1733 www.nycbestbar. com/3SheetsSaloon	Fries with bacon, cheese and gravy are just one reason to check this place out. With three floors, it's great for organizing a group. It's got that good time college vibe.
Daily 11 a.m.–4 a.m.	212-677-6700 www.thunderjack- sons.com	Grab a ninety six ounce Das Boot of beer if you dare! They like their food specials and are convincing when offering up new drinks to try. Try whatever is on sale like $1 hotdogs. Always fun.
Mon–Wed, Sun 11:30 a.m.– 12 a.m. Thu–Sat 11:30 a.m.– 3 a.m.	212-663-7010 www.toastnyc.com	Toast defines farm fresh comfort food. Everything tastes just picked and portions are generous and reasonably priced. Craft beers and very reasonable wine list. I love their huge omelettes during brunch on weekends.

	WHAT	DEAL	LOCATION
344	**Toast** Restaurant & Bar (2 locations)	5 p.m.–8 p.m. daily $1 off drinks	3157 Broadway (between La Salle & Tiemann Place) Cathedral Pkwy (1) MORNINGSIDE HEIGHTS
	House-cured salmon and pork, sixteen beers on tap, $7 beer flights		
345	**Tom and Jerry's** Bar	5 p.m.–7 p.m. Monday–Friday $5 drafts & well	288 Elizabeth Street (between Prince & Houston Streets) Bleecker St (4, 6, 6X) Broadway–Lafayette St (B, D, F, M) 2 Av (F) NOHO
	Cash only, jukebox, FREE bar nuts (sometimes)		
346	**Tribeca Grill** Restaurant & Bar	5 p.m.–7 p.m. Monday–Friday ½ price beer & wine ½ price menu	375 Greenwich Street (at Franklin Street) Franklin St (1, 2) Canal St (A, C, E) Chambers St (1, 2, 3) TRIBECA
248	Extensive wine list, good for special occasions		

HOURS	CONTACT	365 EXTRAS
Mon–Wed, Sun 11:30 a.m.–12 a.m. Thu–Sat 11:30 a.m.–3 a.m.	212-662-1144 www.toastnyc.com	Toast defines farm fresh comfort food. Everything tastes just picked and portions are generous and reasonably priced. Craft beers and very reasonable wine list. I love their huge omelettes during brunch on weekends.
Daily 12 p.m.–4 a.m.	212-260-5045	Great after work spot where one drink can turn into several in the blink of an eye. They have a nice specialty drink and beer list. The booths can get crowded, but everyone is usually having a blast so move in and have a few.
Mon–Thu 11:30 a.m.–10:30 p.m. Fri 11:30 a.m.–11:30 p.m. Sat 5:30 p.m.–11:30 p.m. Sun 11 a.m.–10 p.m.	212-941-3900 www.myriadrestaurantgroup.com	Partially owned by Roberto DeNiro, this place attracts an upscale crowd. The menu features American food and homemade ice cream that is worth the calories. The centrally located bar is a great spot to see and be "scene".

WHAT	DEAL	LOCATION
347 **Trinity Place** Bar & Restaurant	4 p.m.–6 p.m. Monday–Friday $4 drafts $6 champagne	115 Broadway (between Cedar & Thames Streets, enter on Cedar) Wall St (4, 5) Cortlandt St (N, R) Fulton St (4, 5) FINANCIAL DISTRICT
$2–$5 bar snacks, seasonal cocktail menu		
348 **Triple Crown** Restaurant & Ale House	4 p.m.–7 p.m. Monday–Friday $5 domestic drafts $6 drink specials	330 Seventh Avenue (between 28th & 29th Streets) 28 St (1, 2) 34 St–Penn Station (1, 2, 3) 23 St (1, 2) CHELSEA
Irish classics menu, improv and comedy shows		
349 **Trump Bar** Bar & Restaurant	4 p.m.–7 p.m. Monday–Friday ½ price martinis $4 bottles $5 drafts $6 wine $7 well	725 Fifth Avenue, Trump Tower (between 56th & 57th Streets) 5 Av/59 St (N, Q, R) 5 Av/53 St (E, M) 57 St (F) RADIO CITY/ ROCKEFELLER CENTER
250 $23 three-course dinner with FREE glass of wine or draft beer		

MONICA DINATALE

HOURS	CONTACT	365 EXTRAS
Mon–Fri 3 p.m.–11 p.m.	212-964-0939 www.trinityplacenyc.com	You'll feel totally swanky as you enter this old bank vault. It is filled with Wall Street types after the market closes during the week but closed on weekends.
Daily 9 a.m.–4 a.m.	212-736-1575 www.triplecrownnyc.com	This classic Irish pub is friendly and good for soccer fans. Not as crowded as some Penn Station area bars yet still close. You can rent the bar downstairs for parties or sporting events.
Daily 12 p.m.–10 p.m.	212-836-3200 www.trumpbar.com	Even Trump offers a deal in Trump Tower! This lovely, cozy, and posh bar has an extensive martini list and a small appetizer menu to snack on. I love the chocolate martini. The Trump Grill offers dinner specials.

	WHAT	DEAL	LOCATION
350	**Twins Pub** Bar	Daily $3 drafts $5 margaritas	421 Ninth Avenue, #1 (between 33rd & 34th Streets) 34 St–Penn Station (1, 2, 3, A, C, E) 28 St (1, 2) MADISON SQUARE GARDEN/ PENN STATION
	Jukebox, sports specials		
351	**Turtle Bay NYC** Bar & Restaurant	Mon: $1.50 well & $5 pitchers, 5 p.m.–10 p.m.; Tue: $2 PBR; Wed: $1 mugs, $10 pitchers, $.50 wings & $2 sliders; Thu & Fri: ½ price bar & apps, 6 p.m.–9 p.m for $5	987 Second Avenue (between 52nd & 53rd Streets) Lexington Av/53 St (E, M) 51 St (4, 6, 6X) 59 St (4, 5, 6, 6X) MIDTOWN EAST
	Check website for special events and guest bartending.		
352	**Valhalla** Bar & Restaurant	12 p.m.–Close $5 beer specials 1 a.m.–2 a.m. daily $.50 wings 1 a.m.–4 a.m. daily $5 American craft beers	815 Ninth Avenue (between 53rd & 54th Streets) 50 St (A, C, E, 1, 2) 59 St–Columbus Circle (1, 2, A, B, C, D) HELL'S KITCHEN/ MIDTOWN WEST
252	Thirty five plus craft beers on tap, cask beer		

HOURS	CONTACT	365 EXTRAS
Mon–Sat 8 a.m.–4 a.m. Sun 12 p.m.–4 a.m.	212-564-7288	$5 pints of Guinness are hard to come by. A very good pick if you are going to The Garden. The back dining room is less noisy if you want to chill and have a meal.
Daily 12 p.m.–4 a.m.	212-223-4224 www.turtlebaynyc.com	Philadelphia Eagles fans favor this bar with $20 unlimited drafts and wings during the game. Deals, deals, deals. $15.95 brunch on Sundays includes unlimited mimosas or Bloody Marys.
Daily 12 p.m.–4 a.m.	212-757-2747 www.valhallabarnyc.com	If you're looking for a nice craft beer selection and good appetizers, this place will fit the bill. Beer specials and visiting breweries are listed online, and the crowd is a mix of locals and police from the precinct nearby.

| --- | --- | --- |
353 **Verlaine** Asian Tapas & Bar	5 p.m.–10 p.m. daily $3 Yuengling $5 lychee martinis, sangria, Bloody Marys & wine	110 Rivington Street (between Essex & Ludlow Streets) Delancey St (F) Essex St (J, M, Z) 2 Av (F) LOWER EAST SIDE
Large martini and spirits menu, poetry readings		
354 **Village Pourhouse** Sports Bar & Restaurant (2 locations)	5 p.m.–7 p.m. Monday–Friday $2 Bud & Bud Light Drafts Buy-1-get-1-FREE specialty cocktails $10 Bud Light pitchers	64 Third Avenue (at 11th Street) Astor Pl (4, 6, 6X) 3 Av (L) 8 St–Nyu (N, R) EAST VILLAGE
Check the website for special events and tons of drink and food specials.		
354 **Village Pourhouse** Sports Bar & Restaurant (2 locations)	12 p.m.–7 p.m. Monday–Friday $2 Bud Light drafts Buy-1-get-1-FREE specialty cocktails	982 Amsterdam Avenue (at 108th Street) Cathedral Pkwy (1) 103 St (1) Cathedral Pkwy (110 St) (A, B, C) UPPER WEST SIDE

MONICA DiNATALE

HOURS	CONTACT	365 EXTRAS
Mon–Sun 5 p.m.–1 a.m. Tue–Wed 5 p.m.–2 a.m. Thu–Sat 5 p.m.–4 a.m.	212-614-2494 www.verlainenyc.com	The décor is stunning with tall ceilings, red accents and a zen mood. I go for the lychee martinis. The menu is Southeast Asian tapas and includes the Verlaine summer rolls with apple and mint.
Daily 11 a.m.–4 a.m.	212-473-2830 www.villagepour-house.com	Perfect beer halls with twenty plus beers on tap, extensive "global" beer list, and high quality pub grub, including my favorites, the sliders. Because of all their specials, it's a great place to catch up and watch a game.
Daily 11 a.m.–4 a.m.	212-979-BEER (2337) www.villagepour-house.com	

	WHAT	DEAL	LOCATION
355	**Vintage** Lounge	10 p.m.–7 p.m. Monday–Friday, Until 9 p.m. Saturday, Sunday all day $3 domestic beers $3 well & wine $6 Cosmos	753 Ninth Avenue **(between 50th & 51st Streets)** **Bar & Lounge** **50 St (A, C, E, 1, 2)** **49 St (N, Q, R)** HELL'S KITCHEN/ MIDTOWN WEST
	One hundred martinis		
356	**Welcome to the Johnsons** Bar	Until 9 p.m. daily $2 PBR $3 well	23 Rivington Street **(between Essex & Norfolk Streets)** **Delancey St (F)** **Essex St (J, M, Z)** **2 Av (F)** LOWER EAST SIDE
	Jukebox, pool table		
357	**Whiskey River** Bar	3 p.m.–8 p.m. Monday–Friday $3 –$4 drafts $4 well $4 beer of the month $10 bucket of 6 beers of PBR or Nattie Light	575 Second Avenue **(between 31st & 32nd Streets)** **33 St (4, 6, 6X)** **28 St (4, 6, 6X)** MURRAY HILL
	Wii Bowling Tuesdays, fireplace		

MONICA DiNATALE

HOURS	CONTACT	365 EXTRAS
Daily 11:30 a.m.– 4 a.m.	212-581-4655	Dark, sexy and loungey in a Middle-Eastern kind of way. This must be the largest martini list in Manhattan. There are so many, it's hard to choose! I like the chocolate covered banana martini.
Mon–Fri 3:30 p.m.–4 a.m. Sat–Sun 12 p.m.–4 a.m.	212-420-9911	It's a 1970's-retro dive bar complete with fake wood paneling. If $2 PBR is your thing, this is the bar for you. Very grungy with loud music and characters at large.
Daily 3 p.m.–4 a.m.	212-679-6799	Beer pong and skee ball are the main attraction here. The back room is my favorite part with skylights, a fireplace and a TV. It's so bright you may need sunglasses!

	WHAT	DEAL	LOCATION
358	**Whiskey Tavern** Bar	4 p.m.–7 p.m. Monday–Friday $3 Miller Lite $4 Bud Light $6 apple martini & Cosmos $12 pitchers	79 Baxter Street **(between Walker & White Streets)** **Canal St (J, N, Q, R, Z, 4, 6, 6X)** CHINATOWN
	Backyard patio , DJ Fridays and Saturdays		
359	**Whiskey Trader** Bar & Lounge	Daily $5 martinis & shots Until 8 p.m. Tuesday, Saturday, Monday, Tuesdays all day $3 Bud Light pint	71 West 55th Street **(between 5th & 6th Avenues)** **57 St–7 Av (F, N, Q, R)** **7 Av (B, D, E)** RADIO CITY/ ROCKEFELLER CENTER
	FREE popcorn, HD TVs, fireplace		
360	**Whitehorse Tavern** Bar	Daily $3 pints & well $3.50 Guinness $5 PBR & shot	25 Bridge Street **(between Broad & Whitehall Streets)** **Whitehall St (N, R)** **South Ferry (1)** **Bowling Green (4, 5)** FINANCIAL DISTRICT
258	Outdoor seating, jukebox		

HOURS	CONTACT	365 EXTRAS
Daily 11 a.m.–4 a.m.	212-374-9119 www.whiskey-tavernnyc.com	If you're looking for a heart stopper, try the bowl o' bacon. They of course have a nice selection of the "brown" liquor. Try the pickleback shot even if you don't like pickles!
Daily 11 a.m.–4 a.m.	212-582-2223 www.whiskeytrad-ernyc.com	The fireplace room with leather couches makes me feel at home. It combines sports bar, lounge and dance club in the heart of Midtown. A nice affordable option in this area.
Mon–Tue 8 a.m.–1 a.m. Wed–Fri 8 a.m.–4 a.m. Sat 10 a.m.–11 p.m.	212-668-9046	It's one of those places with great history and a corner location that make it very inviting. This is a great place to grab a sandwich and affordable drinks every day. Low key, friendly and full of conversation.

	WHAT	DEAL	LOCATION
361	**Wicked Willy's** Bar	Monday all day, 4 p.m.–7 p.m. Tuesday–Thursday $1 beer	149 Bleecker Street (at LaGuardia Street) Broadway–Lafayette St (B, D, F, M) Spring St (A, C, E) W 4 St (A, B, C, D, E, F, M) THE VILLAGE
	Live music, karaoke, DJs, check events calendar online		
362	**Woody McHale's** Bar & Grill	1 p.m.–7 p.m. Monday–Friday, 12 p.m.–9 p.m. Saturday–Sunday $3.75 domestic & bottled beer $4.50 well $12.50 bucket of Yuengling	234 West 14th Street (between 6th & 7th Avenues) 8 Av (L) 14 St (A, C, E, 1, 2, 3) THE VILLAGE
	$20–$25 wings/sliders and beer all-you-can-eat menus		
363	**WXOU Radio Bar** Bar	3 p.m.–8 p.m. Monday–Thursday, 1 p.m.–8 p.m. Saturday $4 beer & well	558 Hudson Street (between 11th & Perry Streets) Christopher St 0 Sheridan Sq (1,2) 14 St (1, 2, 3) 8 Av (L) THE VILLAGE
	Jukebox, cash only		

MONICA DiNATALE

HOURS	CONTACT	365 EXTRAS
Daily 4 p.m.–4 a.m.	212-254-8592 www.wickedwillys.com	Imagine beer pong, rowdy crowds and karaoke in a pirate ship with neon signs. It's that kind of fun! Local live music Fridays and Saturdays.
Mon–Tue 12 p.m.–2 a.m. Thu 12 p.m.–3 a.m. Fri–Sat 12 p.m.–4 a.m. Sun 12:30 p.m.–2 a.m.	212-206-0430 www.woodymchales.com	It feels like a cabin with it's weathered wood floors but acts like a sports bar. So comfortable you'll want your slippers. Food specials like $2 sliders make it even better.
Mon–Fri 3 p.m.–4 a.m. Sat–Sun 1 p.m.–4 a.m.	212-206-0381	Definitely a friendly and clean dive bar full of Village locals. I love the no Red Bull policy. If you want a neighborhood gem and reasonable prices this is it. No food and no sequins allowed.

	WHAT	DEAL	LOCATION
364	**Yuca Bar** Latin Restaurant	1 p.m.–8 p.m. Monday–Friday $6 sangria $7 margaritas, wine & mojitos; Sunday ½ price tacos & quesadillas; Until 8 p.m. Tuesday ½ price tapas	111 Avenue A (at 7th Street) 1 Av (L) 2 Av (F) Astor Pl (4, 6, 6X) EAST VILLAGE
	$16 weekend brunch includes one FREE drink and rice and beans.		
365	**Zengo** Latin/Asian Restaurant & Bar	5 p.m.–7 p.m. Monday–Friday $4 beer $6 wine $8 cocktails	622 Third Avenue (between 40th & 41st Streets) Grand Central–42 St (4, 5, 6, 6X, 7, 7X, S) GRAND CENTRAL/ MURRAY HILL
	Pick up spice rubs to take home.		

MONICA DiNATALE

HOURS	CONTACT	365 EXTRAS
Mon–Wed 11 a.m.–12 a.m. Thu 11 a.m.–1 a.m. Fri 11 a.m.–2:30 a.m. Sat 10 a.m.–2:30 a.m.	212-982-9533 www.yucabarnyc.com	The ceviche makes me come back for more! Try the pisco passion martini. The atmosphere is absolutely lively and inviting. Affordable tapas menu and good sangria. A good date spot.
Mon–Fri 11:30 a.m.–2:30 a.m. Mon–Wed, Sun 5 p.m.–10 p.m. Thu–Sat 5 p.m.–11 p.m.	212-808-8110 www.richardsandoval.com/zengony	The shrimp ceviche is mouth watering. The elegant dining room has an upscale dinner menu well worth the splurge for any special occasion. The upstairs bar is more intimate. La Biblioteca is downstairs. Special occasion restaurant.

PIZZA, HOT DOGS & DESSERTS

I would be remiss if I didn't include some of the tastiest and cheapest New York City foods. For less than $5, pizza, hot dogs and desserts can brighten any day and fit every budget.

PIZZA

To be honest, I love pizza and haven't had a bad slice in Manhattan. I do find when traveling anywhere else, the pizza simply does not live up to New York pizza. You can ask one hundred different people for the best slice and you will probably get one hundred different answers. Ask around, look around, and you're sure to find your own favorites. That being said, here are three that I like. You can try a pie from each one!

Cheesy Pizza
2640 Broadway (at 100th Street)
212-662-5223
UPPER WEST SIDE
www.cheesypizza.com

I've enjoyed many a late night slice here. Big, floppy and always hits the spot.

Joe's Pizza 7 Carmine Street (between 6th Avenue & Minetta Lane) 212-366-1182
THE VILLAGE
www.joespizzanyc.com

Joe's has been featured in many movies over the years. Quintessential NYC slice. There is no seating, only high tops to enjoy your slice before heading back out into the city. In a great Village neighborhood.

Justino's
881 Tenth Avenue (between 57th & 58th Streets)
212-582-1222
HELL'S KITCHEN/MIDTOWN WEST

Always unique slices available here at this small location, but just enough room to order. No seating.

451 Third Avenue (between 31st & 32nd Streets)
212-686-1211
MURRAY HILL
www.justinospizza.com

Larger location with table seating.

HOT DOGS

Hot dog places in New York are always packed day and night. At less than $3 for a meal, I can see why. These are my picks. The "Papayas" also serve an array of fruit drinks with lots of combinations that contain...papaya.

Gray's Papaya
402 Sixth Avenue (at 8th Street)
212-260-3532
MURRAY HILL

2090 Broadway (at 72nd Street)
212-799-0243
UPPER WEST SIDE
www.grayspapayanyc.com

Nathan's
761 Seventh Avenue (at 50th Street)
212-767-8347
HELL'S KITCHEN/MIDTOWN WEST

705 Eighth Avenue (at 50th Street)
800-628-4267
HELL'S KITCHEN/MIDTOWN WEST

1 Penn Plaza
212-268-5971
(in PENN STATION/ near MADISON SQUARE GARDEN)

401 Seventh Ave (on 33rd Street between 6th & 7th Avenues)
212-630-0327
CHELSEA

1286 Broadway (at Broadway & 33rd Street)
212-630-0315
MURRAY HILL

57 First Avenue (at 4th Street)
212-777-7511
EAST VILLAGE
www.nathansfamous.com

Papaya King
179 East 86th Street (on 3rd Avenue)
212-369-0648
UPPER EAST SIDE
www.papayaking.com

DESSERT

I am a dessert fanatic and when my cravings get out of control, these are my "go to" places. Without breaking the bank, you'll experience your own personal piece of heaven. Any of these places will make your knees weak.

Crumbs Bake Shop
www.crumbs.com

With twenty plus locations in Manhattan, Crumbs specialty is enormous cupcakes that come in fifty plus flavors. I love The Elvis with banana frosting and peanut butter chips, Cookies & Cream and Baba Booey, chocolate and peanut butter heaven. They always have a cupcake of the month and are constantly adding new flavors.

Levain Bakery
167 West 74th Street (at Amsterdam Avenue)
212-874-6080
UPPER WEST SIDE

2167 Frederick Douglass Boulevard (between 116th & 117th Streets)
646-455-0952
HARLEM
www.levainbakery.com

Blink and you could miss it, if not for the lines out the door. Cookies are the specialty here and I'll get whatever is warm! The word cookie simply doesn't do them justice. They are about two inches tall, chunky and slightly gooey. Pure perfection. Yes, they sell bread too!

Magnolia Bakery
www.magnoliabakery.com

Magnolia became famous after being featured in the TV show "Sex And The City." There are five locations in Manhattan including the original at 401 Bleecker Street. For a classic chocolate or vanilla cupcake, they are the best, and maybe better than mom used to make! Even if you don't think you like banana pudding, give theirs a try. It is simply amazing.

Molly's
228 Bleecker Street (between Carmine & Downing Streets)
212-414-2253

THE VILLAGE
www.mollyscupcakes.com

I love that you can "make your own" by choosing your cake and frosting combination. The brown butter frosting is delicious, as are their other center-filled cupcakes like crème brulee and kahlua. If you need more, go to the "sprinkle station" to make your treat just right.

Peanut Butter & Co.
240 Sullivan Street (between Bleecker & West 3rd Streets)
212-677-3995
THE VILLAGE
www.ilovepeanutbutter.com

My love for peanut butter is so deep that I can't look at an open jar without devouring it! What makes Peanut Butter & Co. special is their variety of flavors like White Chocolate Dreams, The Heat Is On and Mighty Maple. For $5-$8 you can bask in the glow of a peanut butter sandwich unlike anything you've tried before. I love the Elvis stuffed with bananas, honey & bacon. Yum. For dessert try the Death by Peanut Butter Sundae or a milkshake like the PB&J Shake. Take a jar home for late night snacking!

SPRING and SUMMER

Chelsea Brewing Company Bar/Restaurant
59 Chelsea Piers (at 18th Street)
212-336-6440
12 p.m.–10 p.m. daily
CHELSEA
www.chelseabrewingco.com

This twelve thousand square foot microbrew-ery has beautiful views of the Hudson River and a sixty slip Marina. The main room has a glass wall and offers outdoor dining in good weather. They make twenty different brews and you can call to arrange a brewery tour. The menu offers great bar food and burgers. Pier 59 is also home to a driving range, a bowling alley and an indoor ice rink.

Pier I Café and Klatch Espresso Bar
Bar/Restaurant
500 West 70th Street and Riverside Park South (enter the park at 66th Street and follow the stairs down)
212-362-4450
Opens May 1st to mid-October, weather de-pending
12 p.m.–11 p.m. Monday–Friday
11 a.m.–11 p.m. Saturday –Sunday

Klatch Espresso Bar
8 p.m.–5 p.m. Monday–Friday
8 p.m.–4 p.m. Saturday–Sunday
UPPER WEST SIDE
www.piericafe.com

Wrought iron tables and colorful umbrellas make this open air restaurant along the Hudson River a gem, especially as the sun goes down. Pier I offers an impressive array of appetizers, salads, sandwiches and entrees including grilled fish and skirt steak. The burgers and Cajun fries alone are worth the visit. Try the red or white sangria by the glass or pitcher, or another drink from the full bar.

The Boat Basin Café Bar/Restaurant
West 79th Street and the Hudson River
212-496-5542
Opens late March/early April through the end of October
  12 p.m.–11 p.m. Monday–Wednesday
  12 p.m.–11:30 p.m. Thursday–Friday
  11 a.m.–11:30 p.m. Saturday
  11 a.m.–10 p.m. Sunday
UPPER WEST SIDE
www.boatbasincafe.com

You will feel like you are at the beach at this indoor/outdoor restaurant. Walk as far west as you can on 79th Street, underneath the overpass, and down the stairs. Open air patio overlooks the Marina with stunning sunset views. You won't believe you're in New York City. No reservations except for private parties. They have great sandwiches and burgers in addition to entrees that include salmon and sirloin steak. The Boat Basin offers picnic table dining and is good for kids.

The Frying Pan Bar/Restaurant
Pier 66 Maritime, West 26th Street, Hudson River Park
212-989-6363
  12 p.m.–12 a.m. daily
  Opens mid–April to October
CHELSEA
www.fryingpan.com

It's almost like entering a movie set as you approach these three floating ships. If you are looking for unique atmosphere, this is it. Find a seat on one of the many decks with spectacular views of the Hudson River at sunset. The menu includes crab cakes, burgers, mini-pizzas and seafood dinners. On weekends after 10 p.m. a DJ transforms the ship into a club with dancing.

The Water Club Seafood Restaurant/Bar
500 East 30th Street (East River between 28th
& 32nd Streets, cannot enter from 30th Street)
212-683-3333
Tuesday–Saturday
  12 p.m.–3 p.m. lunch
  5 p.m.–11 p.m. dinner
Sunday
  11 a.m.–3 p.m. brunch
  5:30 p.m.–11 p.m. dinner
UPPER EAST SIDE
www.thewaterclub.com

The Water Club offers upscale dining with fresh
seafood and meats with entrees ranging from
$26–$41. They are open all year and during the
summer there are two outdoor terraces for casual
drinks. They can host parties of any size and have
beautiful water views of the East River. It is a great
option for any special occasion.

FALL and WINTER

Bierhaus German Restaurant & Bierhaus
712 Third Avenue (between 44th & 45th
Streets)
212-867-BEER (2337)
  11:30 a.m.– 2 a.m. Monday–Wednesday
  11:30 a.m.– 4 a.m. Thursday–Friday
  11:30 a.m.– 2 a.m. Saturday
  12 p.m.– 2 a.m. Sunday
MIDTOWN EAST
www.bierhausnyc.com

Bierhaus offers twenty four German beers on

tap and a full menu to enjoy Oktoberfest in fall. The Wurst Sampler for $24 is perfect for sampling four different sausages. It is located only three blocks from Grand Central Station and tons of fun.

Carmine's Italian Restaurant/Bar
200 West 44th Street (between 7th and 8th Avenues)
212-221-3800
TIMES SQUARE
  11:30 a.m.– 11 p.m. Monday
  11:30 a.m.– 12 a.m. Tuesday, Thursday & Friday
  11 a.m.– 12 a.m. Wednesday & Saturday
  11 a.m.– 11 p.m. Sunday

2450 Broadway (at 91st Street)
212-362-2200
UPPER WEST SIDE
  11:30 a.m.– 11 p.m. Sunday–Thursday
  11:30 a.m.– 12 a.m. Friday – Saturday
www.carminesnyc.com

Carmine's offers delicious Italian family-style dining at a reasonable price. The platters are very large for sharing. During Christmas Carmine's is always very festive and beautifully decorated. They handle the crowds well, but I recommend a reservation.

Eli's Manhattan & Taste Restaurant and Wine Bar
Restaurant/Wine Bar
1411-1413 Third Avenue (between 80th & 81st Streets)
212-717-9798
Monday–Friday
  7 a.m.– 3:30 p.m. breakfast & lunch
  6 p.m.– 11 p.m. dinner
Saturday–Sunday
  8 a.m.– 3 p.m. brunch
  6 p.m.– 11 p.m. dinner
UPPER EAST SIDE
www.elizabar.com

If you are looking for authentic Jewish delicacies for Passover or Hanukkah, Eli's should be your first stop. The twenty thousand square foot store offers house-made breads, coffees and prepared foods. You'll find latkes, brisket and smoked sturgeon. Taste Restaurant uses the fresh ingredients from Eli's and offers a full dining menu and self-service breakfast and lunch.

Lederhosen German Wurst & Bierhaus
39 Grove Street (between Bleecker and Bedford Streets)
212-206-7691
12 p.m.– 12 a.m. Tuesday–Saturday
1 p.m.– 10 p.m. Sunday
THE VILLAGE
www.lederhosennyc.com

You can choose from eight draft and twenty different bottled German beers at this Village find. For $60 you can tap your own mini-keg, or for $25, fill a two liter boot. Food is reasonably priced and worth a visit, especially for Oktoberfest.

Rolf's German Restaurant/Bar
281 Third Avenue (at 22nd Street)
212-477-4750
12 p.m.– 10 p.m. for dining,
Bar open as late as 12 a.m.– 4 a.m.
FLATIRON/GRAMERCY
www.rolfsnyc.com

No one decorates for the seasons like Rolf's. The decorations hang so low and heavy you can hardly see the ceiling and at Christmas you'll feel that you're sitting in a Christmas card. Drink specials change with the seasons as well. You'll find gluhwein and eggnog at Christmastime and traditional brews during Oktoberfest. The German menu includes sausages and potato pancakes. It gets packed so try to arrive before 5 p.m. or after 9 p.m. A must see.

Zum Schneider Restaurant & Biergarten German
Restaurant & Biergarten
107 Avenue C (at 7th Street) 212-598-1098
> 5 p.m.– 2 a.m. Monday–Thursday
> 4 p.m.– 4 a.m. Friday
> 1 p.m.– 4 a.m. Saturday
> 11 a.m.– 12 a.m. Sunday

LOWER EAST SIDE
www.zumschneider.com

Zum Schneider features twelve German beers on tap, seasonal specials and a full German dining menu. Everything is authentic making it the perfect place to celebrate Oktoberfest or watch The World Cup. It is cash only.

ALL SEASONS

Little Italy
Mulberry Street (between Canal & Spring Streets)
www.littleitalynyc.com

Little Italy is home to fifty plus restaurants and cafés. During Christmas it is a festive place to walk the streets and wander into one of the many restaurants. Overall the food in Little Italy is very good. You will find the mostly Italian wait staff extremely friendly as they try to lure you into their establishments. Some of my favorite places include **Grotta Azzurra** (177 Mulberry Street), **La Mela** (167 Mulberry Street) and **Da Nico** (164 Mulberry Street). Da Nico offers a beautiful outdoor garden during the warmer months. La Mela is best for family-style dining at reasonable prices. Try ordering off menu, just ask for "the works" and see what happens! Grotto Azzurra always offers homemade pasta choices. You can check the website to see what festivals are going on as well. The most popular is The

Feast of San Gennaro in September. The streets are blocked off and dozens of food vendors line up. No visit to Little Italy is complete without having dessert at **Ferrara's Bakery & Café** (195 Grand Street), where homemade desserts, gelato and martinis are worth the wait.

Restaurant Row
West 46th Street (between 8th & 9th Avenues)
www.restaurantrownyc.com

Because of the proximity to Times Square and The Theatre District, Restaurant Row offers prix-fixe menus 365 days a year! You don't have to see a show to take advantage of the wonderful discounts. I like **Lattanzi** (361 West 46th Street) and **Bistecca Fiorentina** (317 West 46th Street) for delicious Italian food and **Sangria 46** (338 West 46th Street) delivers outstanding Spanish tapas and Sangria.

Restaurant Week
Twice annually, two weeks each
www.nycgo.com

Restaurant Week occurs twice a year for several weeks in summer and winter. Hundreds of New York City restaurants offer prix-fixe menus for $25 for lunch and $38 for dinner. It is the best way to try cuisine at otherwise pricey restaurants. You will find that many places extend the menus for additional weeks every season. It is best to check the website for a full list of participating restaurants.

365 GUIDE INDEX

INDEX BY NEIGHBORHOOD / LANDMARK LISTING

Yuca Bar

EMPIRE STATE BUILDING
NEAR FIFTH AVENUE AT 34TH STREET

East Pacific Pan-Asian Bistro
Empire Room
Keens
Legends
Rattle N Hum
The Australian NYC
The Ginger Man

FINANCIAL DISTRICT
**THE SOUTHERN TIP OF MANHATTAN
INCLUDING WALL STREET &
BATTERY PARK CITY**

Adrienne's Pizza Bar
Beckett's
Iron Horse NYC
Killarney Rose
Mad Dogs & Beans
O'Hara's
Ryan Maguire's Ale House
Smorgas Chef (Stone Street)
Suspenders
The Beekman
The Dubliner
Trinity Place
Whitehorse Tavern

FLATIRON/GRAMERCY
**14TH STREET TO 29TH STREET,
SIXTH AVENUE TO FIRST AVENUE**

Arctica
Barbounia
Barfly
Bocca
Bull's Head Tavern
Copper Door Tavern
Crema
Dewey's Flatiron
Duke's (19th Street)
ilili

Manhattan Brewhouse
No Idea Bar
Old Town Bar
Parea Bistro
Pranna
Punch Restaurant & Wined Up
Rodeo Bar
Rogue
Slate
Spin
The Globe
The Hog Pit
The Mad Hatter
The Pizza Pub
The Trailer Park Lounge
The Watering Hole

GRAND CENTRAL
**NEAR 42ND STREET
BETWEEN MADISON, PARK
& LEXINGTON AVENUES**

Calico Jack's Cantina
Cellar Bar
Darbar
La Biblioteca
McFadden's
Naples 45
Overlook
Snafu Bar
Zengo

GREENWICH VILLAGE
SEE THE VILLAGE

HARLEM
SEE ALSO MORNINGSIDE HEIGHTS

**WEST HARLEM:110TH TO
155TH STREET, MORNINGSIDE
AVENUE TO HUDSON RIVER**

**CENTRAL HARLEM: 110TH STREET
TO 157TH STREET, FIFTH AVENUE
TO ST. NICHOLAS AVENUE**

EAST HARLEM: 96TH STREET TO HARLEM RIVER, EAST RIVER TO FIFTH AVENUE

Dinosaur Bar-B-Que (west)
El Paso Restaurante (3) (east)
Harlem Bar-B-Q (central)
Lenox Lounge (central)
Moca Lounge (central)
Shrine (central)

HELL'S KITCHEN/ MIDTOWN WEST

34TH STREET TO 59TH STREET, EIGHTH AVENUE TO HUDSON RIVER

123 Burger Shot Beer
Arriba Arriba
Bamboo 52
Bar Nine
Barcelona Bar
Bourbon Street Bar & Grill
Chelsea Bar & Grill
Disiac Lounge
El Azteca
Empanada Mama H.K.
Gaf West
Hallo Berlin
Holland Bar
Il Punto
Kennedy's
Lansdowne Road
Lincoln Park Grill
Lucky Strike Bowling
McCoy's Bar
Mercury Bar
Riposo 46
Rudy's Bar & Grill
The House of Brews (51st Street)
The Pony Bar
The Snug
Valhalla
Vintage

INWOOD

DYCKMAN STREET TO NORTHERN TIP OF MANHATTAN, HARLEM RIVER TO HUDSON RIVER

Garden Café
Guadalupe
Indian Road Café
Mamajuana Café

LINCOLN CENTER

NEAR WEST 62ND STREET TO 66TH STREET, BETWEEN AMSTERDAM & COLUMBUS AVENUES

Ed's Chowder House
The Empire Hotel Rooftop

LITTLE ITALY

CANAL STREET TO HOUSTON STREET, BOWERY TO LAFAYETTE STREET

BarBossa
Botanica Bar
Brinkley's Broome Street
Café el Portal
L'asso (Mott Street)
Milano's Bar
Onieal's
Oro Bakery & Bar
Red Egg

LOWER EAST SIDE

CANAL STREET TO EAST HOUSTON STREET, EAST RIVER TO FORSYTH STREET

169 Bar
Barramundi
Boss Tweeds Saloon
Cake Shop
Epstein's Bar
Fontana's Bar
Georgias Eastside BBQ
La Caverna
Lolita

Loreley
Móle (Allen Street)
Nurse Bettie
Parkside Lounge
San Marzano
Schiller's Liquor Bar
The Sixth Ward
The Ten Bells
The Whiskey Ward
Verlaine
Welcome to the Johnsons

Gyu-Kaku (Third Avenue)
Jameson's
Keats
Murphy's Pub
Opal
Pig 'n' Whistle (Second & Third Avenues)
Redemption
Snafu Bar
The Irish Exit
The Stag's Head
Turtle Bay NYC

MADISON SQUARE GARDEN/PENN STATION

NEAR 4 PENN PLAZA AT 8TH AVENUE & 31ST STREET

Blaggards Pub & Restaurant
Blarney Rock Pub
Blarney Stone
Brother Jimmy's BBQ (Eighth Avenue)
Foley's
Jack Dempsey's
Mustang Harry's
Mustang Sally's
Stitch
Twins Pub

MIDTOWN

SEE EMPIRE STATE BUILDING, MADISON SQUARE GARDEN/PENN STATION, RADIO CITY MUSIC HALL/ROCKEFELLER CENTER

34TH STREET TO 59TH STREET, EIGHTH AVENUE TO FIFTH AVENUE

MIDTOWN EAST

42ND STREET TO 59TH STREET, FIFTH AVENUE TO EAST RIVER

Ashton's Alley
Cellar Bar
Copia
Cornerstone Tavern

MIDTOWN WEST

SEE HELL'S KITCHEN, TIMES SQUARE/THEATER DISTRICT

MORNINGSIDE HEIGHTS (WEST HARLEM)

110TH STREET TO 155TH STREET, ST. NICHOLAS AVENUE TO HUDSON RIVER

1020 Bar
Amsterdam Restaurant & Tapas Lounge
Havana Central (Broadway)
Paddy's
The Heights Bar & Grill
Toast (3157 Broadway)

MURRAY HILL

29TH STREET TO 42ND STREET, SIXTH AVENUE TO EAST RIVER

Bar 515
Brother Jimmy's BBQ (Lexington Avenue)
Cask Bar & Kitchen
Docks Oyster Bar
Duke's (Third Avenue)
El Parador Café
La Biblioteca
Pine Tree Lodge
Slattery's
Terroir (Third Avenue)
The Whiskey Rebel
Third and Long

Whiskey River
Zengo

NOHO

Broadway to Bowery, Astor Place to East Houston Street

Aroma Kitchen & Winebar
Bleecker Street Bar
Five Points
Great Jones Café
Sliánte
Swift Hibernian Lounge
The Spring Lounge
Tom and Jerry's

PENN STATION

See Madison Square Garden

PORT AUTHORITY

See Times Square/Theater District

RADIO CITY MUSIC HALL & ROCKEFELLER CENTER

Near West 50th Street, Between Fifth Avenue & Avenue of the Americas (Sixth Avenue)

Johnny Utah's
McCormick & Schmick's
Pazza Notte
Pig 'n' Whistle (West 47th)
Trump Bar
Whiskey Trader

SOHO

Vesey Street to West Houston Street, Lafayette Street to Hudson River

Ear Inn
Emerald Pub
Emporio
Gatsby's

Hundred Acres
I Tre Merli
Lucky Strike
Lure Fish Bar
Papatzul
Puck Fair
The Cupping Room Café

SOUTH STREET SEAPORT

Peck Slip to John Street, Pearl Street to South Street

Acqua at Peck Slip
Cowgirl Sea-Horse
Fresh Salt
Jeremy's Ale House
Meade's Bar

THE VILLAGE

14th Street to West Houston Street, Broadway to Hudson River

8th Street Wine Cellar
1849
Agave
Amity Hall
Apple Restaurant and Bom Bar
Art Bar
Barrow Street Ale House
Bayard's Ale House
Betel
Blind Tiger Ale House
Corner Bistro
Do Hwa
Down The Hatch
Dublin 6
Entwine
Fiddlesticks
Fish Restaurant
Galway Hooker
Greenwich Treehouse
Gusto
Johnny's Bar
McKenna's Pub
Mercadito (Grove Street)
Móle (Jane Street)

Oliver's City Tavern
Panca
Shade
Slane Public House
Smorgas Chef (12th Street)
Spunto
Sweet Revenge
The Dove Parlour
The Four-Faced Liar
The Half Pint
The Mermaid Inn (MacDougal Street)
The Village Tavern
Three Sheets Saloon
Thunder Jackson's
Wicked Willy's
Woody McHale's
WXOU Radio Bar

TIMES SQUARE/ THEATER DISTRICT

NEAR 42ND STREET & SEVENTH AVENUE

RESTAURANT ROW- WEST 46TH STREET BETWEEN 8TH & 9TH AVENUES

Churrascaria Plataforma
Daltons
Dave's Tavern
Gyu-Kaku (44th Street)
Havana Central (46th Street)
Holland Bar
Jimmy's Corner
Langans
Latitude Bar & Grill
Mother Burger
O'Flaherty's Ale House
Pig 'n' Whistle (47th Street)
Playwright Celtic Pub
Smith's
The House of Brews (46th Street)
The Long Room
The Mean Fiddler

TRIBECA

VESEY STREET TO CANAL STREET, BROADWAY TO HUDSON RIVER

B Flat
Churrascaria Tribeca
Dark Horse
Greenwich Street Tavern
Lilly O'Brien's
M1-5
Mudville 9
Nancy Whiskey Pub
Puffy's Tavern
Souths
Terrior (Harrison Street)
The Patriot Saloon
Tribeca Grill

UNION SQUARE

EAST 12TH STREET TO EAST 17TH STREET, BETWEEN BROADWAY & PARK AVENUE SOUTH

Belmont Lounge
Blind Pig
BLT Fish
Brother Jimmy's (16th Street)
City Crab and Seafood Company
El Cantinero
Flex Mussels (13th Street)
Pete's Tavern
Spain
Stand

UPPER EAST SIDE

59TH STREET TO 96TH STREET, FIFTH AVENUE TO EAST RIVER

Baker Street Pub
Bar Coastal
Brandy's Piano Bar
Brother Jimmy's BBQ (Second Avenue)
Cilantro (First & Second Avenues)
Doc Watsons
El Paso Restaurante (2)
Fetch
Flex Mussels (82nd Street)

Index by Type (Casual/Lounges, Pubs/Sports Bars & Restaurants)

CASUAL BARS/LOUNGES

12th Street Ale House
B Side
Barramundi
Belmont Lounge
Botanica Bar
Boxcar Lounge
Brandy's Piano Bar
Brinkley's Broome Street
Broadway Dive
Cake Shop
Cellar Bar
Common Ground
Copia
Corner Bistro
Coyote Ugly
Crocodile Lounge
Dark Horse
Dave's Tavern
d.b.a.
Disiac Lounge
Ear Inn
El Cantinero
Empire Room
Epstein's Bar
Fontana's Bar
Gaf West
Greenwich Treehouse
Hi-Fi
Holland Bar
Iggy's
International Bar
Iron Horse NYC
Jimmy's Corner
Johnny's Bar
Keybar
La Linea
Lenox Lounge

Lolita
M1-5
Meade's Bar
Milano's Bar
Moca Lounge
Nancy Whiskey Pub
No Idea Bar
Nurse Bettie
Old Town Bar
Paddy's
Parkside Lounge
Rodeo Bar
Rudy's Bar & Grill
Ryan's Daughter
Scratcher
Shrine
Smith's
Snafu Bar
Stand-Up NY
Tap-A-Keg
Ten Degrees Bar
The 13th Step
The Empire Hotel Rooftop
The Four-Faced Liar
The Hog Pit
The Library
The Snug
The Spring Lounge
The Underground
The Uptown Lounge
    Restaurant & Bar
The Watering Hole
The Whiskey Rebel
The Whiskey Ward
Tom and Jerry's
Vintage
Welcome to the Johnsons
Whiskey River
Whiskey Tavern
Whitehorse Tavern
WXOU Radio Bar

PUBS/SPORTS BARS

2A
123 Burger Shot Beer
1020 Bar
1849
Amity Hall
Amsterdam Ale House
Amsterdam Tavern
Art Bar
Baker Street Pub
Bar 515
Bar Coastal
Bar Nine
Barcelona Bar
Barfly
Barrow Street Ale House
Bayard's Ale House
Beckett's
Blaggard's Pub & Restaurant
Blarney Cove
Blarney Rock Pub
Blarney Stone
Bleecker Street Bar
Blind Pig
Blind Tiger Ale House
Blondie's
Boss Tweeds Saloon
Bourbon Street Bar & Grille
Brother Jimmy's BBQ
Bull McCabe's
Bull's Head Tavern
Burp Castle
Chelsea Bar & Grill
Copper Door Tavern
Cornerstone Tavern
Croxley's
Daltons
Dempsey's
Dewey's Flatiron
Dive 75
Dive Bar
Doc Watsons
Down The Hatch
Dublin 6

East Village Tavern
Emerald Pub
Fetch
Fiddlesticks
Finnerty's
Flight 151
Foley's
Galway Hooker
Gatsby's
George Keeley Fine Ales & Lagers
Greenwich Street Tavern
Jack Dempsey's
Jack Russell's Pub
Jake's Dilemma
Jake's Saloon
Jameson's
Jeremy's Ale House
Johnny Utah's
Karma
Keats
Kennedy's
Killarney Rose
Kinsale Tavern
Langans
Lansdowne Road
Latitude Bar & Grill
Legends
Lilly O'Brien's
Lincoln Park Grill
Lion's Head Tavern
Loreley
Lucky Strike Bowling
Mad River Bar & Grille
Manhattan Brewhouse
Manny's On Second
McAleer's Pub & Restaurant
McCoy's Bar
McFadden's
McKenna's Pub
McSorley's Old Ale House
Mercury Bar
Merrion
Molly Pitcher's Ale House
Mother Burger
Mudville 9

RESTAURANTS

Apple Restaurant and Bom Bar
Arctica
Arriba Arriba
Aroma Kitchen & Wine Bar
Ashtons Alley
Asia Roma
B Flat
Back Forty
Ballarò Caffé Prosciutteria
Bamboo 52
BarBossa
Barbounia
Betel
BLT Fish
Bocca
Café el Portal
Calico Jack's Cantina
Cask Bar & Kitchen
Churrascaria Plataforma
Churrascaria Tribeca
Cilantro
City Crab and Seafood Company
Cleopatra's Needle
Cowgirl Sea-Horse
Crema
Cucina Di Pesce
Darbar
Dinosaur Bar-B-Que
Do Hwa
Docks Oyster Bar
Duke's
East Pacific Pan-Asian Bistro
Ed's Chowder House
El Azteca
El Parador Café
El Paso Restaurante
Empanada Mama H.K.
Emporio
Entwine
Esperanto
Fish Restaurant
Five Points
Flex Mussels
Fresh Salt
Fulton

Garden Café
Georgias Eastside BBQ
Great Jones Café
Guadalupe
Guayoyo
Gusto
Gyu-Kaku
Hallo Berlin
Harlem Bar-B-Q
Harry's Burritos
Havana Central
Hearth
Hundred Acres
I Tre Merli
ilili
Il Punto
Indian Road Café
Keens
Kefi Restaurant
Klong
K-One/KTV
L'asso
La Biblioteca
La Caverna
Locksmith Wine Bar
Lucky Strike
Lure Fishbar
Mad Dogs & Beans
Mamajuana Café
Maya
McCormick & Schmick's
Mercadito
Móle
Naples 45
Opal
Oro Bakery & Bar
Panca
Papatzul
Parea Bistro
Pazza Notte
Planet Sushi
Pranna
Punch Restaurant & Wined Up
Red Egg
Riposo 46

INDEX FOR WEEKEND DEALS

The Sixth Ward
The Ten Bells
The Thirsty Scholar
The Trailer Park Lounge
The Uptown Lounge
    Restaurant & Bar
The Village Tavern
The Whiskey Rebel
The Whiskey Ward
Third and Long
Three Sheets Saloon
Toast
Twins Pub
Valhalla
Verlaine
Vintage
Welcome to the Johnsons
Whitehorse Tavern
Whiskey Trader
Woody McHale's
WXOU Radio Bar

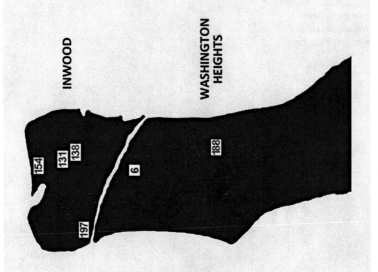

INWOOD

WASHINGTON
HEIGHTS

154

131

138

197

6

188

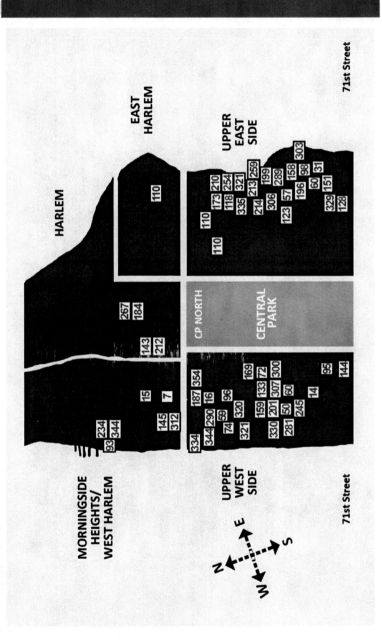

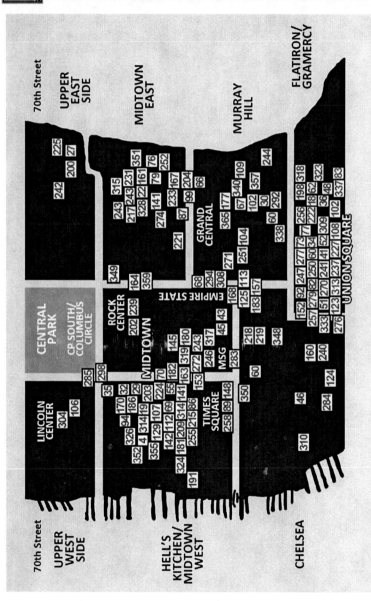

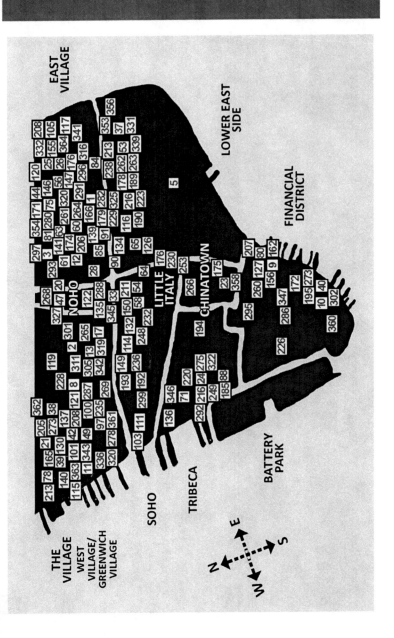

EAST VILLAGE

THE VILLAGE WEST VILLAGE/GREENWICH VILLAGE

SOHO

TRIBECA

NOHO

LITTLE ITALY

CHINATOWN

LOWER EAST SIDE

FINANCIAL DISTRICT

BATTERY PARK

N W E S

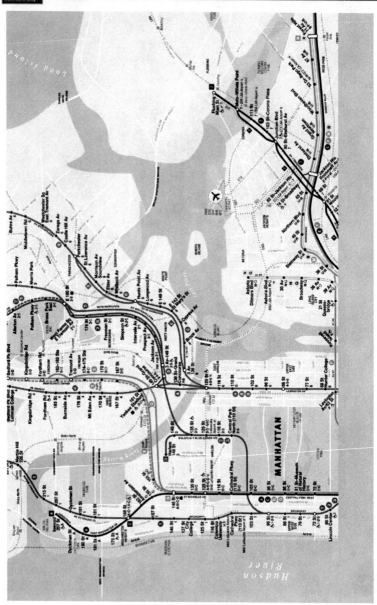

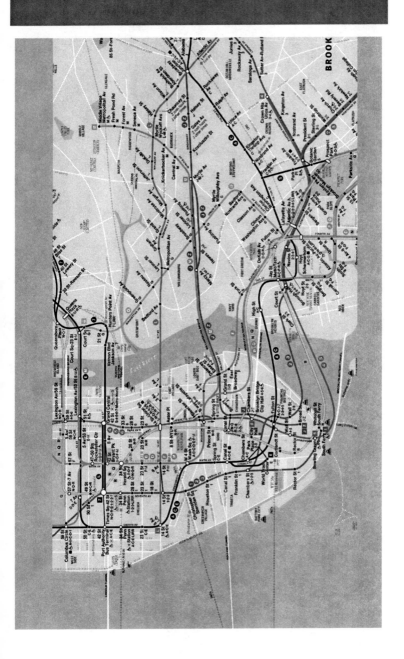

CPSIA information can be obtained at www.ICGtesting.com
Printed in the USA
BVOW04s2238131113

336220BV00010B/202/P

9 781936 449477